Praise for JP Infante & *On the Tip of Your Mother's Tongue*

"These paragraphs remind me that growing up often seems like an initiation into secrets—just learning them but understanding which ones to share and which to keep."
—Yuka Igarashi, executive editor of Graywolf Press

"JP Infante captures the complexities of addiction, homelessness, mental illness, and racial identity through the lens of a son whose mother is dedicated to one thing: survival. *On the Tip of Your Mother's Tongue* is a lesson in snapshot vulnerability and introspection. Infante moves us rapidly through short scenes condensed with an emotional precision that forces us to slow down and contend with our own disasters. Whether on the tip of a tongue, or an iceberg, the magic in this book is in what lives underneath, every word that has yet to be said."
—Elisabet Velasquez, author of *When We Make It: A Nuyorican Novel*

"In 'Without a Big One,' JP Infante provides the reader with a glimpse at the impact of incarceration on black and brown families. This powerful short story also touches upon issues of love, poverty, education, and mental health, all through the lens of one young child in Washington Heights.
Prison reform and prison abolition are receiving increased mainstream attention, and as readers, we see the harm done to the family at the center of 'Without a Big One.' Community intervention has its place. Cages do not. Infante's art helps to move us away from these cages and closer to a more just and equitable society."
—Laura Pegram, founder & publisher of *Kweli Journal*

"It is a rare feat to personify a city as grand as New York. Seeing it through the gritty realism lens of lived experience; JP Infante has done this twice. This book can illuminate on a digital billboard or be stapled onto a light pole."
—Josh Dale, editor-in-chief, Thirty West Publishing House

ON THE TIP OF YOUR MOTHER'S TONGUE

SELECTED WORKS

JP INFANTE

Thirty West
Publishing

10 YEARS
2015-2025

ISBN-13: 979-8-9895422-7-7
Cover photograph © 2016 "High Hopes", Roy Baizan
Jacket design by Josh Dale
Edited by Josh Dale & Nadia Jackson
Translations by Liz Lugo, Francis Mateo, Roxana Calderón
Printed in the U.S.A.

For more titles and inquiries, please visit:
www.thirtywestph.com

Amberlyn aka Mati

"My normal way of being is really to support, encourage, praise, feed, take care of everyone who comes into my household. But if because of oppression, discrimination, abuse, disrespect, I lose the equilibrium that I need to do this function— which is very innate— then I cannot be this being that I am here to be. And so, when you think of all the women, mothers, in the world who are just not only not supported but are actively being ground into the dirt. It's no mystery that the world is in the shape that it's in."

—Alice Walker

TABLE OF CONTENTS

On the Tip of Your Mother's Tongue

UMBILICAL

1.

You rushed out of school where she waited. You looked up at her and smelled liquor.

As you crossed the street you told her about Mr. Castro and how he threatened to whip any boy who fought in class.

She held your hand and frowned. "I'll cut him," she said. Screeching tires stopped everything. The car almost hit you. She yanked your shoulder and yelled, "The light is yellow!" The driver rocked in the car, gripping the steering wheel.

She let go of your shoulder when you reached the sidewalk. Her grip. Your bruise. You weren't scared of the driver or Mr. Castro but for them.

2.

Before you exited Rikers you got your belongings from the lockers. The bus was packed with mothers, sisters, daughters, little boys, and summer heat. Somebody upset someone because a seat belonged to someone. The large woman shouted at your mother. Your mother tossed your month-old sister at you and faced the large woman's chin, screaming back louder.

The bus driver pleaded with the women, struggling with the wide steering wheel. You thought the driver would take your mother back to jail for fighting, but that was only fear. You didn't fear jail or the large woman, you feared dropping your sister.

3.

This was before your sister, before a lot of things. You lived in an apartment with a woman and her small child. Mice slept under a mountain of toys in the living room. A worm-like tail slipping through action figures, doll hair, and stuffed animals.

You don't remember the kitchen, the bathroom, or the woman your mother rented from. You remember your small bedroom and the blue walls. There was a broken window and a cold radiator by the twin-size bed.

Throughout the night you trembled in her arms. In the morning you put on your hat, coat, and gloves for school and yet still felt a chill slip through the window cracks inside. You couldn't tell if you were scared or cold or if there was a difference.

BUYING COCAINE

1.

Bring an Afro-Latino or Black friend with you.

Don't confuse your Spanish friends with your Spanish-speaking friends. Your dealer has never been to Spain and will pretend he doesn't know English if two white guys approach him. Your dealer thinks white is white the same way you think black is black. Your dealer won't overcharge you if you're with a non-white person.

2.

I'm lying. This isn't about you.

Your dealer will overcharge you not because you're white, but because you can afford it. This neighborhood is no different than that resort you went to in the Caribbean. Your dealer is more American than you think. He's an aspiring capitalist just like those third-world resort workers.

Platanos with Salami. Brugal with Coca-Cola. That light purple juicy warm hole inside that dark pitch-black woman.

You were overcharged there. You will be overcharged here.

3.

Focus on the coke.

When you get off the George Washington Bridge, you'll be on 178th Street and Fort Washington by the bus terminal. It will look like the U.N. You'll see brown, white, and black junkies from all over the world. This ain't *Bright Lights, Big City*. This is real cosmopolitanism. The neighborhood is made up of Americans, including law-abiding undocumented citizens. Forget them.

4.

Drive down 178th Street and make a left on Wadsworth Avenue. Ignore the merengue spilling out of windows and reggaeton left over from cars flying by. Ignore the people on plastic chairs in front of tenement buildings, drinking and celebrating God knows what on St. Nicholas Avenue. Throw your 50 Cent CD out of the car window. Ironically playing a 50 Cent CD you paid for proves your whiteness and does not camouflage you.

5.

Be yourself. Be white.

Don't be like those dealers on the corner. It won't help in any way. The truth is that these dealers love whiteness more than you or they could ever understand. Read *Black Skin, White Mask* by Frantz Fanon or Wilhelm Von Schadow's chapter summaries in *Liberator Magazine.*

6.

Avoid walking by the church. If you pass by on foot the churchgoers will notice when you forget to cross yourself. Plus, they'll know you weren't there last Sunday. For them, it's about community and charity and you are an outsider that hasn't donated.

7.

While looking for parking you'll discover a university for a specific group of people is a block away from your dealer. Park your car in front of George Washington High School. The dropout rate is as high as the property tax money going into the school is low.

8.

Don't be surprised if you see people you identify with. Rent is more expensive than ever so a lot of us are moving out. Rent is cheap. Consider moving to the area.

9.

Mayor Giuliani cleaned the city but his hands ain't clean. His soldiers used a plunger on a Haitian immigrant while they protected and served. Fortunately, you're far from a dark skin Haitian so you're safe.

10.

Don't badmouth the last dealer who sold you the flour that ain't numb your tongue. Most of these dealers have dealt with each other and if they haven't they will. A few of them are more industrious than you, investing in laundromats until the dryer stops spinning, the money's clean, and the laundromat becomes a local business like an actual laundromat. Most of the corner dealers are already in jail. Some of these blocks are traps, smaller than small towns. Read Sherwood Anderson's *Winesburg, Ohio,* and James Joyce, *The Dubliners.*

11.

When you get to your dealer's block avoid Terrence. He's around your age. He can tell you're white and not Eastern European and he holds this against you. He read *A Small Place* by Jamaica Kincaid and is still angry. He's in that prestigious school that didn't accept you even though both of you had identical grades. You'll roll your eyes and blame Affirmative Action. Terrence will suck his teeth and counter with Legacy Preferences.

12.

Don't smile at Josefina. She'll be waiting in front of your dealer's building for her father to pick her up. Josephina's father, the taxi driver, does nothing except work, read the newspaper, and drive his daughter around. He only knows baseball. He's never played golf and thinks Tiger Woods is a place in upstate New York and yet owns a four iron. Stay away from his daughter. He's old school and was oppressed in the days when blatant oppression was in style. He'll hack you with his golf club as if St. Nicholas Avenue was that puddle of a river dividing Hispaniola and you've mispronounced a Spanish word. Read Edwidge Danticat's *The Farming of Bones.*

13.

You'll find the dealer waiting for you on the third floor. When you tell him I sent you, he'll take out the coke. Do not tell him how you know me or ask him how he knows me. He counts the money repeatedly and you grow anxious. You fear he'll rob you like the last dealer from the hood you last scored at. He won't small talk. He won't tell you he's dealt to my mother behind my back, but this story isn't about that.

When he finally gives you the stuff, you'll feel relieved and jokingly ask how much cut is in it? The dealer will remind you that nothing is pure.

ALMOST ALL ABOUT YOUR MOTHER

You were seven or eight the first time you questioned your mother's sanity. Before entering a Human Resources Administration office in Washington Heights, she said, "If they ask, tell them I'm crazy." To this day you're not sure if she was joking.

This was back in the day before EBT cards. You looked like siblings, an older sister with her brother, applying for food stamps. The HRA worker was a tall skinny Black woman with glasses. Your mother thought food stamp eligibility required applicants to be crazy. You were torn because you knew—even at that age—that kids were taken away from crazy parents.

While the HRA worker questioned your mother you waited to be asked about her sanity. You thought hard about the question. Thinking about it now as you write this, you question if you ever knew your mother. You remember her sleeping a lot. She played music late into the night causing arguments with neighbors. She complained about bills and yet managed to buy you whatever toys you asked for. Your mother answered the HRA worker's questions while you waited to be asked, "Is your mother crazy?" You were never asked. Maybe because sanity wasn't a requirement for food stamps or because the answer was known.

The women in your family: great grandmother, grandmother and mother are mostly silent about their past, saying little to the men in the family: your maternal uncle and you. However, when they're hurt and angry they remind each other of the pain they've caused each other. The women in your family have always been a mystery to the men in your family. These women are known, but only to each other.

During an argument between your mother and grandmother you learned your mother had been placed in a Colombian Presbyterian psych ward at 14. You can't remember what the argument was about, except that your mother swore she would never forgive her mother for forcing her into a place for crazy people.

You never thought your mother was crazy— not because she's your mother— but because anytime she claimed to be or acted like it, there was some ulterior motive. One time she played crazy to get a new apartment.

When you were a teenager, your great-grandmother and you went to visit your mother at her apartment in the Bronx. She hated this apartment and had been trying to move because of poor maintenance and neighborhood gang violence. When you got to the building, the neighbors told you your mother was in the hospital after her apartment caught on fire.

At the hospital you were told she was in the psychiatric ward because they suspected her of arson. Your great-grandmother and you were concerned until you saw your mother. She had made friends with the security guards, doctors, and patients in the unit. She introduced you to everyone. The contrast between your mother's energy and the other patient's lethargy and slurred speech convinced you she wasn't crazy.

After some paperwork, your great-grandmother signed her out.

On the way home in the cab she said, "It was a little fire. I'll get a nicer place."

You asked, "Why were the people there so slow?"

"The pills," she said, "I pretended to swallow the ones they gave me."

Your mother was right. She got her new apartment after the fire.

The summer before you turned 28 you visited your mother at a psych ward in Queens Lebanon Hospital. This time she wasn't trying to get money from some social program or an apartment or sympathy from the family. She complained that her ex, a big-time drug dealer, had people prank calling and following her. At the time you weren't sure if she was acting crazy. It didn't matter. She had typecasted herself. Your mother kept taking on the same role.

The psych ward unit was on a high floor. The visiting

room's window showed a vast landscape of Queens with the sun sinking behind the Manhattan skyline. Your mother smiled, telling you she wanted to stay two more days to calm her nerves. She wasn't crazy just stressed. As your mother talked a young man walked towards you too. At first you thought he was Dominican like you, but learned he was Egyptian and that he had a crush on your mother. He introduced himself and declared his love for your mother. You all laughed. He said he was only 21 but would treat her right. He was charming and good-looking. Your mother told him you were a writer, so he began telling you an idea he had for a novel. The story would be about mermaids forced to live on land and move around in wheelchairs. He asked if you were religious and you said, "barely Catholic." He said your mother would have to surrender to Islam if they got married. You all laughed. He recited a verse from the Quran and even though you didn't understand you appreciated the musicality. You asked him about his family. His mother had died recently after years of battling cancer. He said his father used to be a good man. He said if he married your mother, he would be a lenient stepfather. You all laughed.

You were reassured your mother wasn't crazy and concluded the young Egyptian was trying to cope with his mother's death but was close to losing it completely.

As your mother walked you out, she whispered, "What do you think?"

"About what?" you said.

"About marrying the guy? He's from a good family."

You looked at your mother unsure if she was joking. You asked, "Are you serious?"

She kissed you and said, "I'll call you tomorrow."

On the way home on the 7-train, you realized your mother wanted your blessing and felt like crying. You hadn't cried in years. Whenever you felt the urge, your mother's voice played in your head, something she once told you: "When a man cries for me, I lose respect for him."

That night seeing your reflection on the train window, superimposed over a Queens landscape and New York City skyline under a starless night, reminded you of that time she lost her train of thought. You immediately recognized what she was trying to remember in her eyes and the sight hurt like a kick inside your stomach; it was your name on the tip of your mother's tongue.

WITHOUT A BIG ONE

You've thought about jumping.

It's a cold winter night. You sit next to Queeny on your fire escape. The cars on the freeway come and go like waves. The lights from the George Washington Bridge reflect off the Hudson River like the shine in glassy eyes. The river is a giant bathtub without a ship or boat to save anyone who might be drowning. Your babysitter, Nilda, says suicide is like killing someone, and if you were to survive jumping off the fire escape, the police would arrest you for attempted murder. If you do try killing yourself, you plan to live through it because suicide only works if you survive. Nilda laughed when you told her the attempt was meant to get people's attention. She laughed because it's true. You feel the frigid wind. Look at the buildings across the river in New Jersey. They are far apart with too much space in between. There's no space between you and Queeny because you both need warmth.

They used to call you Minene, and before that, Chungo, even though your birth certificate says another name. Your stepfather, who's been away at school for three months, calls you son. Son, get me the TV controller. Son, listen to your mother. Son, stop talking about your heart.

Your stepfather can draw you and your extra small heart. Queeny is asleep at your feet. He can draw anything and anybody. He knows everything about sports, anime, video games, comic books, and toys. He's the strongest man you've met and the only man who has ever kissed you. He has never lied. When he turned himself into school you felt like crying, but didn't, because you've never seen him cry.

Mary gave birth to you. She calls you Minene or Ray and sometimes your stepfather's name by mistake. Mary doesn't hear it when you call her mom. She calls you Raymond when Queeny plays with her shoes or does poo in the house. Mary doesn't love Queeny like your stepfather. Mary is younger than all your friends' mothers. Mary looks young like your babysitter, but you know Nilda's younger because she's happier than your mother.

Sometimes you sleep with Mary in the bedroom. You like rubbing her hair on your nose. Sometimes the smell of shampoo and cigarettes makes you sleepy. Sometimes the mix keeps you up at night. You usually sleep on the sofa bed in the living room because of your bladder disease. Recently it's been hard to hold your piss at night.

Your new doctor says *Konnichiwa* all the time. He said kids who drink soda wet the bed and Mary believed him. You don't trust this doctor because when you asked if he was Chinese, he pointed to a red circle at the center of a white rectangle and said Japanese. Then he smiled at Mary.

One night you fell asleep with Mary in the bedroom and her snoring woke you around midnight. The TV showed old men talking about bladder disease. The next morning at the kitchen table, you told Mary about bladder disease. She was shuffling mail, knife in hand. She stopped, looked at the bowl in front of you, and said, Mentiroso before cutting open a red envelope in one try. She usually doesn't speak Spanish, so you didn't understand her. The way Mary pronounced that word made her a stranger.

That morning you realize the Chinese doctor was flirting with her. You make a mental note to tell your stepfather when he calls from school. He's only called a couple of times since he left because the apartment phone is always being cut off and there are never minutes on Mary's prepaid cell phone.

Your babysitter, Nilda, calls you Ray Ray. She loves Queeny. Nilda is taller than Mary and has a fat ass. Whenever you hug her, you touch it, and she doesn't say anything. Nilda is in love with you. You don't tell her you know because she has a boyfriend. Every time Nilda sees you, she laughs, but not at you, it's just she's embarrassed by being in love with someone your age. At night in bed, you imagine kissing Nilda and licking her lips.

Nilda is smart and Nilda is beautiful, and Nilda reads you stories with curse words and words you don't understand. She says you're mature. She says you should draw your drawings instead of tracing. One day, Nilda told her friend with the huge boobs you'll be a heartbreaker. Her friend asked, "Would you be my boyfriend?" It took a while to answer because you didn't want to hurt Nilda's feelings. You blurted out, It depends, and Nilda's friend laughed. Nilda barely giggled because she was jealous. That day you knew you had to make it up to her. So, when Nilda asked for a drink, you put ice in her ginger ale. And when you gave her the soda you saw her face through the glass and Nilda looked like she was made from gold.

Nilda reminds you of your homeroom teacher Mrs. Vicioso because she doesn't *paternize*. It is a word Nilda taught you. When she caught you tracing your stepfather's sketches Mrs. Vicioso said, "You can do better."

Your stepfather sketched Big Ralph, the supermarket owner from New Jersey who is always eating. Anytime Ralph tells you something he ends it with, Know what I mean, Jellybean? Ralph is scary because he's bigger than that gorilla you saw in the zoo. His breathing sounds like he just climbed up the stairs even if he's been sitting in a chair. Sometimes while standing he nods off. It looks like he's gonna fall on his ass and never get up.

Nilda called Ralph a Glue-Ton once. She says the word comes from the Latinos in Greece and it means "to swallow." Nilda says Latino is a language that's dead because it killed itself or someone killed it. You're not sure how Latinos made it to Greece, but Mrs. Vicioso says they live all over the world because of Spain. You know the word means more than "to swallow." It has to do with someone who can't get enough of something, but you can't remember what Nilda said.

Ralph used to bring shopping bags full of food from his supermarket before your stepfather left for school. The fridge has been emptied since then, and you haven't seen Ralph. You have seen Nilda's secret friend, Gregorio. You almost forget about him because Nilda said not to tell anyone when he comes around. You don't like Gregorio because when he visited, he only paid attention to Nilda. You went to trace your stepfather's drawings and fell asleep on the sofa.

Today you wake up to the smell of piss and alcohol. Not the perfume the wannabe doctor rubbed on you, but the one Mary smells like. Did you wet the bed? Feel your underwear. Take them off. The faded Superman looks normal. Dry. Put your clothes on for school. Mary is not awake to make you shower.

Today is different. You won't walk the long way through boring Riverside Drive or climb up a mountain hill to Fort Washington Avenue. Today you'll take the shortcut with your best friend Frankie even though your stepfather told you not to take the short way without him.

Frankie calls you Ray Ray like the rest of your classmates. When the two of you walk to school, he talks nastier than a cockroach-filled radio. You two always take the long way because the shortcut takes you under George Washington Bridge through a pathway of broken glass and needles. Where zombies live. Frankie says zombies smoke crack. He knows all this because he has two older brothers. One is away at college, like your stepfather, and the other is in jail for having weed.

Frankie decides to wait until after school to take the shortcut. After school, you meet Frankie and follow him through Fort Washington Park. He ignores the other kids on the monkey bars and swings. You notice two empty swings, but Frankie doesn't stop. Ask yourself if you're scared. Are you scared? The thought of taking the shortcut without your stepfather makes you wanna pee. You pass the dog pen and wonder what Queeny's doing. Some dogs bark, others sniff around and the rest run in circles.

Frankie sits on a bench that faces New Jersey when you reach the back entrance of the park. He starts talking about two airplanes crashing into George Washington Bridge and ends up talking about his brother calling from Rikers.

"Is he scared of jail?" you ask.

"Nope. It's only the skinny guys who get raped."

Are you scared of taking the shortcut?"

Frankie doesn't answer. He kicks a diaper down the stairs.

You remember your house phone might be back on, so you stand and exit the park. You rush down the stairs that lead to the freeway. Shattered glass crunches like cornflakes with each step. You almost slip on frozen garbage. You make it to the sidewalk next to the freeway and see a large brown box under the scaffolding between George Washington Bridge and the buildings on Riverside Drive.

"There's a shoe coming out of the box over there," says Frankie.

Pick up a plastic bottle. Throw it. The bottle bounces off and rolls down the cracked pavement. The shoe doesn't move.

"Shit Ray Ray, he's dead," says Frankie.

Frankie and you collect whatever bottles and rocks aren't smeared with shit. Wait. 1...2...3 Attack! Bottles shatter and rocks dent the box. Stop. The laughing ends and the hum of speeding vehicles on the freeway and the bridge return. The box stands still.

Walk on the sidewalk by the freeway. There's a path that diverges into the street that leads to your building on Riverside Drive. The cars pass fast and close to this narrow path, so you walk under the scaffolds where the zombies live. The scaffolds are part of an abandoned construction next to the bridge. There are broken handrails, burnt benches, and dirt with cracked pavement. A zombie folds a garbage bag big enough for two bodies. He smiles at you.

"That crackhead keeps looking at us," says Frankie. The two of you turn around before walking any closer to the zombie with the giant garbage bag. You walk back the long way home. When you reach the stairs that lead to Fort Washington Park you notice there's no shoe coming out of the brown box.

"He's not there 'cause he's alive," says Frankie.

"Let's see what's inside."

Pick up a bottle. Frankie is behind you. Glance at the stairs that lead to Fort Washington Park and the dog pen and your school and everything safe. Touch the cold cardboard. Listen. Meowing. Look through a hole while holding your nose. No cats. Turn around and a few feet away a zombie in a ripped black sweater has a rock in his hand. You freeze. Frankie runs up the stairs. The zombie throws the rock. You duck.

Frankie shouts from the top of the stairs. "He's got a knife!"

Worry. Hold the dirty glass bottle with both hands. The zombie walks like he's on a tightrope about to fall. The closer he gets the more it smells like piss and the more you want to pee. You hear someone calling your name. Look up the stairs. Frankie's gone. Look over your shoulder. Feel the frigid wind from the passing vehicles. Imagine your stepfather is watching, waiting to yell at you for taking the shortcut without him. Throw the bottle. It bounces off the zombie's chest. Run up the stairs and take the long way home.

A breeze of shit and piss blows out of the apartment when you push open the door. Mary whips Queeny with your stepfather's belt. Queeny runs to you whimpering with a trail of blood behind her. Every seven months she bleeds. Mary's eyes are swollen like she just woke up or finished crying. She isn't wearing any makeup. The darkness under her eyes looks like shadows. As Queeny trembles between your legs, you realize how ugly Mary's become.

"This dog is gone," yells Mary. "We're getting rid of it today."

Nausea. Hold your nose. All this could be easily cleaned: the drops of blood, the pieces of shoes, the chewed corners on the sofa, the rubble of shit, and the puddles of piss.

"Just clean it," you say.

Mary throws a shoe at you.

You duck and shout, "I hate you."

After hours of crying and threats of running away, you find yourself on Pinehurst Avenue close to where Olivia, a friend of your stepfather, lives. Queeny is on a leash ahead of you and Mary.

"Rich people live around here," says Mary. "They'll adopt her."

Drop the leash. Hope Olivia finds her. Follow Mary. Don't look back. Queeny follows you, dragging her metal leash over the concrete. So, you end up in Fort Washington Park and leave Queeny in the dog pen where she forgets about you and chases after the other dogs.

That night Mary asks if you want to sleep with her.

You say, "I hate you," and lick your lips, tasting the salt from tears and boogers.

"We can't afford that dog. She was starving," says Mary, slamming the bedroom door.

~

Three days have passed, and you haven't killed yourself. Your stepfather hasn't called. Frankie hasn't been to school since the day you attacked the zombie. Mrs. Vicioso says he's sick. You've asked the dog owners in Fort Washington Park about Queeny, but no one has seen a reddish-brown dog with hazel eyes that looks like a bulldog but is really a mutt.

This morning Mary woke you up for school by caressing your face because she knows you're mad about Queeny. She caressed your face at the hospital after almost drowning in the bathtub. You saved her that day by pulling her head out of the water and holding on tight to her hair.

After school you find Nilda sweeping the kitchen. Pass her and go to the living room. Sit on the sofa. Wait for her to say something. She says something. Ignore her. She drags the broom into the living room and stands under the lamp like an angel-witch with a glow over her head.

"I'm sorry about Queeny," she says.

"Queeny's dead."

"You're wrong, Ray. They adopt dogs like Queeny."

"Don't paternize me."

"What?"

"Don't paternize me."

"You mean patronize. Do you think I'm patronizing you?"

"Depends."

You go and sit at the kitchen table and look out the window. Think about jumping out. Nilda throws words at you while cooking spaghetti because it's the only food left.

"Stroke," yells Nilda.

"It's like to strike, but only harder like a punch."

Stirring the pot, Nilda says, "Nope, it's a gentle touch like petting a cat."

"Didn't you say it was a heart attack?"

"Nope," she says with her back to you. "It's a soft touch. Next word… Independent."

"Being single and happy—"

There's a knock on the door. Think about your stepfather. Think about Queeny. Think about Nilda's secret friend, Gregorio. Nilda checks her cell. She turns a knob on the stove and walks out of the kitchen. Think about jumping out the window and breaking one leg.

"Come on, baby, she ain't gonna say shit," says the man in the hallway.

"I can't. It's my job," says Nilda.

"Come on, love."

"Only for a few minutes."

The door closes. Locks click. A man in a Yankee baseball hat extends his hand. Stare at it. He wears a leather jacket, jeans, and black boots. He's younger than your stepfather.

"Hi, Mr. Rodriguez," says the man.

"This is my friend, Nino," says Nilda.

"Yes, her boyfriend," says the man.

Your chest feels funny. Think about your heart murmur. Cavity. Nilda says anything can have a cavity, not only teeth.

"Daydreaming, Mr. Rodriguez?" asks the man with his hand out.

"Stop calling him that," says Nilda. "He's not in the mood."

Her friend, Nino, says he's seen you around. He says most stray dogs are adopted. Ignore him. Walk out of the kitchen with your plate.

You hear loud whispering in the kitchen.

"Are you seriously thinking of going?" asks Nino.

"I'm going," says Nilda. "It has nothing to do with Greg."

"What is it with you and this Greg-guy?"

"Some of my friends are going to be male."

"I ain't bring Gregorio up. Why travel so far?"

"Because I want to," says Nilda in five hard whispers.

Dishes slam in the sink.

Wake up after falling asleep on the sofa. Water runs in the bathtub. Nino sits on the other end. A picture book and a jackknife rest on his lap.

"Mr. Rodriguez," says Nino fixing his belt. "You think keeping a secret is important if it could get someone in trouble?"

Rub your eyes. Don't say anything.

"Would you get me in trouble Mr. Rodriguez?"

You don't understand. Stay shut. He's a stranger.

"Have you ever gone under the bridge?" asks Nino.

"No."

"You sure you haven't gone under the scaffolds?"

"Yea... But with my stepfather. I can't go alone."

"If you snitch, Mr. Rodriguez—"

"Why you call me that?"

"Respect," says Nino. "Nilda says you hate being patronized... I'll get to the point... You ain't tell Nilda you saw me under the scaffolds because you ain't a snitch. If Nilda found out you saw me, she'd think I was doing something wrong. And if I tell your mom I saw you throwing bottles at bums you'll get in trouble. But I ain't a snitch."

Nod because you almost understand. He thinks you saw him taking the shortcut under the bridge.

"You kept a secret. I trust you, Mr. Rodriguez."

Nino flips through the pages of *Where the Wild Things Are.* "Lonely boy surrounded by monsters. Sounds like Beasts of No Nation."

Nino doesn't look like someone who likes books. His hat is now to the back. He's like those guys with red eyes that lean with one foot against the wall and sit on milk crates by the corner. Guys like Frankie's drug dealing brother.

"His mom sends him to bed without supper," says Nino.

"That book is for little kids," you tell him. "You know about heart murmurs?"

"Heart problem?" says Nino, scratching the few hairs on his chin.

"I have one. Mary says I was born with an extra small heart."

"Who's Mary?"

"My mother."

"You look healthy. Nilda said you wanna run away."

"Sometimes."

"Me too," says Nino, "but I wanna run back to my parent's place."

"Why?"

"I got kicked out for selling... for... taking the shortcut."

"I haven't talked to my stepfather in mad long," you say.

"Reading helps you not think about people you miss. You gotta read a lot to be with a girl like Nilda."

Don't believe that Nino reads. He's not like Nilda.

"Imagine you had a girlfriend with a new friend named Gregorio," says Nino. "Now imagine this girlfriend mentions this new friend lent her a boring book called School Days by Patrick-something. And your girlfriend says it's better than the book that you like Beasts of No Nation."

"She thinks that other schoolbook is better than the beast-book?" you ask and try not to think about Nilda's secret friend.

"Yup, that's what Nilda thinks. She's never finished Beasts of No Nation cause it's too violent. I read it and loved it, and I don't even like reading. I never finished School Days because it's boring. I wonder why she likes that boring book, School Days, so much."

"Because it's not violent?"

"No, no, wrong, Mr. Rodriguez. Remember this Gregorio-friend told her about the School Days book." He starts cleaning his nails with the jackknife. "How would you feel if you finally read a book to impress your girl and she doesn't even read the book you read?"

"Jealous because she likes Gregorio's book better."

"Shit, you're smart... Has Nilda talked to you about Gregorio?"

"Nope," you say, rubbing your chest because your heart hurts when you lie but would hurt even more if you snitch. "Is Nilda your girlfriend or your friend?"

"My girlfriend," he mumbles.

"Are you scared that Gregorio is bigger than you?"

Nino laughs. "I'm never scared. He might be taller but not bigger—"

Nilda comes out of the bathroom with her hair messed up. She asks for clean blankets. Nino puts one finger over his lips. You tell her they're dirty. Go to the bedroom. Nilda makes the bed over with the same dirty sheet even though Mary had already made the bed that morning. When she's done you fall on the bed. Underneath one of the pillows is a moist spot that smells like Clorox. Fall asleep.

Fall with Mary. She holds your hand tight. There's a bridge in the sky above. The wind feels like a cold shower. Steam comes out of Mary's mouth because of the cold outside or something deep inside. Fall isn't so bad, and it feels like a rollercoaster ride. As you plummet notice two objects falling below. The two objects grow closer until you drop pass them. Look up. See your stepfather and Queeny floating in the air. Both bodies disappear. You can't find Mary. Try flying. It feels like you're swimming. You're drowning. Swim.

Wake up and smell Queeny. The lamp reflects on the TV screen, where the only clean spot is your handprint in a thick layer of dust. The hamper teems with dirty clothes and a puddle of jeans around it. Shades cover the two fire escape windows. Stretch your legs. It's not Queeny you smell but your own piss. Mary will go mad when she finds out.

Nilda could dry the bed with a blow-dryer. Ever since Nilda surprised Mary with a visit she fixes everything. Nilda was dressed in black slacks and a grey shirt. She wore makeup, her hair was blow-dried and an ID hung around her neck. Nilda wrote in a black notebook and asked about you dialing 911 and saving Mary's life when she almost drowned in the bathtub. At first Mary told you not to tell Nilda anything because she was going to try to take you away. But Nilda helped Mary get food stamps and a sofa bed and babysits whenever Mary goes out.

If Nilda doesn't dry the bed Mary will go mad. Your jeans stick to your legs. You almost shower but change jeans instead. The living room is dim with the kitchen light. Nilda's gone. Mary snores on the sofa like always. She forgot parent-teacher conference is tomorrow. Scratch your tear ducts. The crust goes in your nails. The floor creaks. Bite your nails. Run away because she went crazy the last time you wet the bed. Put your coat on. Look at Mary dreaming before you leave. Grab her by the wrist and touch your face with her hand. Her watch says 11:30 PM. There's a hole in between her nostrils. She coughs and gasps for air. Press on her heart like the ambulance man. She coughs. She doesn't open her eyes like when you pulled her out of the bathtub.

Mary says, "Chris?" but doesn't wake up.

It's nighttime but Riverside Drive is not scary. It's not like morning when there are no parked cars. The yellow in the apartment windows tell you who's awake. Sometimes you can see the shadows of families on walls and ceilings. You cross the empty streets in the dark cold. The winds are angry on Pinehurst Avenue. Stop coughing. You can't. Keep coughing. Boogers run down your stuffy nose. Wish you had a hole between your nostrils like Mary.

Surprise! Ralph is in front of Olivia's building. The fat guy from New Jersey who used to bring food to your house, but disappeared when your stepfather left for school, sits on the stoop with shopping bags. He is nodding off like a zombie. But Ralph is too fat to be a zombie. If Ralph sees you, he'll snitch and tell your stepfather. Run back home.

Run up your building's stairs. Hope your stepfather hasn't called.

Mary blocks the door to the apartment. "Where have you been?"

"Nowhere."

"Want me to tell Chris you ran away because you wet the

bed?"

The cuticles on your middle finger bother you. Bite them off. It burns. "I saw Ralph taking food to Olivia's building."

"What?" asks Mary. "Big Ralph?"

"Yeah."

"Let's go," she says.

When you and Mary get to Pinehurst Avenue, she tells you to stay across the street from Olivia's building. She leaves you her cell phone and tells you to call the cops if anything happens. Mary enters Olivia's building. Wish Ralph was taking food to your house. Think about how the light posts glow the color of pee. Look at the moon. It doesn't look like it's made out of cheese.

Mary runs out of Olivia's building with two shopping bags. "Let's go," she says. "Let me get the phone."

Keep up with Mary as she talks on the cell.

"Answering machine, Ralph? You fat piece of shit. If I find you in the Heights buying from that cutthroat, Olivia, I'm gonna make Chris cut your balls off when he comes out. I could've gotten you what you needed like Chris used to, but you go behind my back to Olivia..."

"Why you mad at Ralph?"

"He's a drug addict," she says. "I don't want you around junkies."

The next morning you wake up alone in the bedroom. Mary didn't wake you up for school, but she never does. You hear a man in the living room. Think about your stepfather.

Nino is on the sofa, talking on his cell. "… I won't throw it in your face. I'm doing the boy a favor not you… Studying abroad ain't about studying. People travel to fuck." Nino sees you, puts one finger on his lips and hangs up.

"Is Mary in the hospital?"

"No, your mom's running errands and Nilda's at work."

"I'm late for school."

"You won't miss nothing it's half day today. Don't tell Nilda I let you stay home…

Hungry? I ordered Chinese for breakfast."

"It's half a day because it's parent-teacher conference today."

"I know," he says. "Nilda and your mom won't be back until later so I'm gonna take you."

Around dusk you and Nino take the shortcut to school. One of the zombie's yells from under the scaffolds, "Arturo!"

Nino throws a hand in the air and says, "Dry."

When you reach the foot of the stairs that lead to Fort Washington Park, you ask Nino, "Why does Nilda help my family?"

"It's her job. Plus, you remind her of her cousin Juan."

"Does Juan have a dog?"

"Nope."

"Did Juan get left back?"

"I don't know. Maybe. Community college is like being left back."

"Was Juan born with a heart murmur?"

"I'm not sure, Mr. Rodriguez."

"Did Juan's mother try to suicide herself?"

"Juan's mother died from taking drugs," says Nino, cleaning his nails with the jackknife.

The moon is out when you reach an empty Fort Washington Park. No runaway kids on the playground or runaway dogs in the dog pen. The swings are so still, they look frozen. You can see right through the monkey bars. There's no line for the big slide. Nino and you sit on a bench by the water fountain because you're early. There are no stars just an airplane's red light in the sky.

"Nilda said she's going to Spain."

"I know." Nino opens his eyes wide like they need air.

"You sell drugs?"

"I know people in jail for selling drugs," says Nino.

"That bum called you Arturo. You got different names for different people?"

"Yup and different secrets," says Nino. "Mr. Rodriguez, if you knew Nilda had another boyfriend would you tell me?"

"Depends."

When you enter school, Nino leaves to talk to Mrs. Vicioso and drops you off at the gym where there are no adults. There are big kids throwing basketballs at smaller children under the bleachers. A girl in a pink coat chokes a girl in a blue coat. A boy runs up to you, screams and then runs away leaving a sneaker behind. Two boys howl at the ceiling lights.

You sit on the bleachers ignoring the kissing sounds below

you and watching everyone's parents drop them off. Frankie enters the gym with his father. His father looks old and stupid because he doesn't know English. Frankie is a liar who abandoned you. Your stepfather would kill Frankie's father in a fight. Frankie's father doesn't care about Frankie because he leaves him behind with all these crazy kids in the gym. Frankie runs across the gym and the closer he gets the more he looks like his father.

"I spoke to my brother," says Frankie. "He's not in Rikers. He's in the S.H.O.C.K. program. Like a boot-camp jail. He saw your father. There's this drill sergeant with a tattoo on his arm of a black baby hanging on a rope that makes them do pushups—"

"He ain't my father. He's my stepfather and he's in college."

"It's not a real college like my other brother is in. They just let them take a test for a diploma."

"Stop lying."

You punch Frankie in the face. He walks backward, crying like a little bitch. Frankie covers his nose with blood dripping between his fingers. He might bleed to death. A crowd forms around the two of you. Run to the backdoor exit. Hurry!

Run across the street to an empty Fort Washington Park. The police will arrest you. Think about drowning in the Hudson River. Run downstairs to the freeway. Pause at the foot of the stairs. On the other side of the eight lanes of freeway is another park and after that is the Hudson River.

Think before crossing. Feel the wind of cars speeding by like they're racing.

Someone grabs your arm. Scream.

"Give me money."

"I don't got nothing."

The zombie puts you in a headlock and presses a cold metal on your throat. He searches your pockets. "I'll rip your heart out."

"I was born with a heart murmur."

Close your eyes. Pray to your stepfather. The zombie flies off you. Nino slams the zombie on the ground. He jumps on the zombie, chokes him with one hand and holds his jackknife with the other.

"Don't stab the zombie, Nino."

Nino looks at you. He looks at the zombie before letting him go.

While on your way home Nino's cell rings.

"Yes, he was in the park," he says. "His mother will call you."

Nino doesn't ask why you punched Frankie.

"Let's make a deal, Mr. Rodriguez. If you don't let Nilda leave for Spain, I promise not to tell anyone about tonight. Deal?"

"OK, but tell me... Is my stepfather in jail for selling drugs?"

"Yeah, Raymond," says Nino and pats your head. "I'm sorry."

Believe Nino. Your stepfather is in jail. You don't want to snitch on Nilda, but you rather be a snitch than hide something from Nino. So, you tell him about Gregorio.

"Mr. Rodriguez, you don't gotta pretend you know Nilda's friend. I won't tell anyone about tonight regardless."

Don't tell Nino anything else about Gregorio because it hurts his feelings. He doesn't believe you because he doesn't want to believe.

The next morning Mary's snoring wakes you in the bedroom. It's Saturday but you don't feel like watching cartoons. On one window the shade is halfway down so you see the dust the sun brings. On the other window the shade is fully drawn so there's no dust. It's better to keep the blinds down because the dust makes you sneeze.

Mary's cell phone vibrates on the floor.

"Hello?"

"Will you accept the collect call from Christian Ruiz?" asks a robotic voice.

"Yes."

"Hello," says a raspy voice.

It sounds like your stepfather is crying. Stay shut. Listen.

"I'm sorry I haven't called," he says. "I didn't want to—"

"Nilda says men cry... You know Queeny is gone?"

"I heard. Is Nilda that Children Services woman?"

"Yeah. She helped Mary get a job, but Mary got sick and lost it."

Your stepfather coughs. "If she's sleeping give her a kiss."

Rub your nose against Mary's and smell cigarettes. Love the smell. Remember how she used to laugh with a cigarette in her mouth, one eye squinting because of the smoke. Touch her lips. The dryness feels like torn plastic. Lick your mother's lips.

"Are you drawing?" he asks.

"Yeah, tracing yours."

"You can't trace my drawings or take the shortcut."

"Are you in jail for selling drugs?"

He clears his throat. "Son, I told you I'm in school."

And even though Frankie, Nino, and the voice inside you all say that your stepfather is in jail, you decide to believe your stepfather.

BACHATA

During the reign of Mayor David Dinkin, my pops
brought home the bacon, out hustling NYPD and making
jewelry out of melted badges he gifted my moms.

Pops brought in the streets in the soles of his
Timberlands
  so moms mopped with Clorox, Fabuloso, and sound.
  She cleaned the sidewalks off our tiles with Whitney
Houston's "I Will Always Love You."

John Gotti's arrest was an omen. A drought soon
followed for 40 days and 40 nights.
  Pops worked overtime late nights doing Christ-work.
  But instead of turning water into wine he turned laxative
and procaine into cocaine, selling "na con na" to know-
nothings.

Giuliani became mayor and pops got home later and
later.
  Moms music changed to La India's "Ese Hombre."
  Til one night pops never made it home.

Mom's friend, a taxi driver, drove us to visit pops upstate
while the radio played bachata.

During pop's bid, mom's music changed again.

Alex Bueno's "Busca un Confidente" was on repeat.

And then a billionaire was elected mayor.

This was years after my pops was released and

long after my parents separated.

I was visiting my mom's crib when a bachata song came
on *La Mega.*

I told her bachata reminded me of her cleaning.

She said it reminded her of the taxi driver—

but then cut herself off with quiet

so we listened to the lyrics instead.

ON SCREENS

"People post Baldwin quotes, but they don't read him."
—Marwa Helal

On March 23, 2024, my stepfather passed away. I'm writing this four months later. The US presidential election has taken over the news cycle. They say democracy hangs on a thread. Russia attacks Ukraine, the United States funds Ukraine. Israel commits a genocide in Palestine, the United States funds Israel. I'm seeing the faces of Palestinian children being dug out of the rubble of bombed buildings. So many dead children, like a horror movie—a screen between me and the genocide.

A year before his death, on May 17, 2023, my stepfather texted me: "Yo, please answer. It's important. I'm in trouble; I need help." That same day, Donald Trump, the front-runner for the 2024 Republican nomination at the time, took credit for the US Supreme Court overturning *Roe v. Wade.* On social media, he posted: "I was able to kill Roe v. Wade." On that same day, Congressman Bill Foster, a Democrat from Illinois, reintroduced the Expanding Opportunities for Recovery Act, which would allow states to be awarded grants through the Center for Substance Abuse Treatment. The money would expand prevention efforts and evidence-based treatments, including medication-assisted treatment. Congressman Foster's press release headline read: "Foster Introduces Legislation to Combat the Opioid Epidemic." Later that day, my sister texted me that my stepfather—her father—needed the money for heroin. I texted back: "I know."

In two months, I'll hit forty. I thought I would be able to make sense of the endless breaking news alerts on my phone or observe without absorbing. But it's the opposite. The closer I get to forty, the more confusing the news, no matter if it's from New York City, Appalachia, Bangladesh, Palestine, the Democratic Republic of the Congo, or Sudan. At night, a need for coherence keeps me up in bed. My mind tries making a one story out of hours of scrolling Instagram, TikTok, and YouTube. Behind my eyelids is a game of chance. A slot machine with three-reel spins. The reels show an erratic assortment of every image I have ever seen, whether with my own eyes or on a screen. There's no jackpot to win as the spinning never stops. No combination of images in my head leads to meaning. I just wake up tired the next day.

Making sense of the daily news cycle is no different than making sense of your life when you realize you have more years behind you than ahead. You can organize the images in your head chronologically to create meaning, but that doesn't guarantee you'll understand anything you saw or lived. The older I get, the more fragmented my autobiographical notes become. I can't tell you if what I remember is a childhood memory, a scene from a movie or a book, or something I saw on some screen. In an essay titled "The Artist's Struggle for Identity," James Baldwin speaks about the life of the poet and the artist. "You survive this and in some terrible way, which I suppose no one can ever describe, you are compelled, you are corralled, you are bullwhipped into dealing with whatever it is that hurt you," he said. At this moment, I can't distinguish the life I've lived from the retrospective screening of events in my mind, an in memoriam of all the people I've known and all the people I've been. How many times have I revised the beginning and ending of my own story?

I get flashbacks of walking down Fort Washington Avenue toward the George Washington Bridge on a brick winter night, ready to fly. I couldn't finish *Another Country* in my first two tries. Today, I think of one of the novel's characters, Rufus Scott, and how he was successful where I failed. Scott is an African American jazz drummer who commits suicide, jumping off the George Washington Bridge. I can't discern my ruminations from that night and Scott's suicide in Baldwin's novel. I remember being dead broke. Then I called my stepfather, who sent me money the following day. We never had an honest conversation about my suicide ideation and his substance use disorder. Even when he congratulated me for a writing achievement, we never discussed the past my fiction was based on, a history we shared.

~

In *The Devil Finds Work*, Baldwin reviews *The Exorcist* (1973). He's not convinced the possessed twelve-year-old girl, Regan, masturbating with a crucifix was a realistic portrayal of evil. He claims the movie prioritizes special effects over actual damnation, writing, :"For, I have seen the devil, by day and by night, and have seen him in you and in me: in the eyes of the cop and the sheriff and the deputy, the landlord, the housewife, the football player: in the eyes of some junkies, the eyes of some preachers, the eyes of some governors, presidents, wardens, in the eyes of some orphans, and in the eyes of my father, and in my mirror." For Baldwin, the movie's depiction of evil ignores the real, unacknowledged evil in American society.

As a kid, I watched horror movies with my parents, but can't recall watching *The Exorcist*. I know the image of the possessed girl levitating from the bed, cursing at priests and playing with the crucifix. Watching as an adult, I laughed when the possessed twelve-year-old told Father Damien Karras, "Your mother sucks cocks in hell, Karras, you faithless slime." Father Karras is tormented by guilt because he wasn't present when his mother passed away alone in a small apartment. In another moment, the demon tells him, "You killed your mother! You left her alone to die! Bastard!" Baldwin writes, "This uneasy, and even terrified guilt is the subtext of *The Exorcist*, which cannot, however, exorcise it since it never confronts it."

I wish I had seen *The Exorcist* with my parents. My twenty-four-year-old mother and nineteen-year-old stepfather let me watch any movie just as long as I whined and begged. If I didn't watch any R-rated movie with them, it wasn't because they were protecting me from the profanity or special effects. It was because I was scared and didn't really want to see it.

I wish they had exposed me to the horrors of their lives, how they let me watch R-rated movies. At eight, I saw what was happening on our side of the screen. No matter what I heard from adults in my family and at school, I only believed what I saw. Mood-altering substances or drugs were all around my neighborhood. They were in my family. Aspirin, coffee, nicotine, etc. Beer and liquor. And yet in the apartment I lived in and the school I attended, I was only told, "Just say no." If someone offered me drugs, I had to just say no. Based on the public service announcements I saw about drugs, I got the impression someone in the street was going to pull me into an alley and force me to do drugs against my will. That never happened. Any drug I've done has been consumed enthusiastically. The last time I fought against taking drugs, I was probably a baby, swiping at medicine on a spoon.

There was no transparency. There was no conversation. Only thing I knew about drugs were the "special effects." I saw alcoholics, junkies, crackheads, *piperos, tecatos.* And I called them these names. Adults called these people these names. I judged the people who weren't strong enough to say no and were now too weak to stop cold turkey and save themselves. As a child, I never recognized those who were "functioning" and consumed out of sight in secret or during weekends. In my mind, when a person failed to say no to drugs, they instantly transformed into someone with a substance use disorder. Casual users, social users, experimenters didn't exist. Drugs were evil. To this day, this is how many adults talk to teenagers about drugs. The instructions are: Don't take drugs. And the solution for those with substance abuse disorder is: Stop using.

By adolescence, I knew my parents used drugs, but I never talked to them about it. They never talked to me about it. For many years, this didn't affect me because you couldn't see it in their eyes. It was a secret. But I knew long before it was obvious. I personally knew what Baldwin meant when he wrote: "Children, not yet aware that it is dangerous to look too deeply at anything, look at everything, look at each other, and draw their own conclusions."

I regret not speaking to them about the reality on our side of the screen as an adult. I never questioned them. I'm aware even if I had faced them as an adult, I wasn't guaranteed the truth or their survival. But like Baldwin said, "Not everything that is faced can be changed, but nothing can be changed unless it's faced."

We rented VHS tapes from the Blockbuster on 178th Street and Broadway. We also rented from a small VHS store on 186th Street and St. Nicholas, where All Star Barbershop is located today. I can't remember where we rented *Faces of Death* (1978). We watched it in my parents' bedroom. I can't remember my parents ever telling me I was too young to watch an adult movie. One time, I put my finger in a sugar jar and rubbed the sugar in my gums. I was imitating Christopher Walken or Laurence Fishburn in *King of New York* (1990). My mother called my stepfather over and asked me to do it again. I refused. They never told me not to do it, but I knew not to do it again. The night we watched *Faces of Death*, I didn't know death. My great-grandmother was alive then. My mother was alive. My stepfather was alive. When I revisited the film recently, I learned it wasn't a documentary. For years, I recommended *Faces of Death* to people as a documentary about dead bodies and people eating monkey brains. I say dead bodies, but I mean faces. Death is in the face. Doesn't matter if someone overdoses, commits suicide, or dies of cancer, or old age. Soon as the heart stops, the face changes. Heavy-handed mortician. Gentle mortician. Makes no difference. There's no mask for death. Many lifetimes after first watching the film, I learned *Faces of Death* is not a documentary, but a mondo horror film. Mondo is a subgenre of exploitive documentary film, sensational pseudo-documentaries made with stock footage and staged scenes. They portray cultures outside the United States, focusing on subjects like death and sex.

For years, I imagined I had gotten a kind of education. I swore *Faces of Death* taught me something about death other ten-year-olds didn't know. What exactly did I imagine? I don't know. I only just learned, two months away from forty, that this movie I have been recommending is not a documentary. I learned this long after my great-grandmother's death in the Dominican Republic. Eight years after my mother passed away in Cali, Colombia. A few months after the death of my stepfather in Jersey City.

For a long time, I thought I knew something about the world that other kids didn't because I watched R-rated movies with my parents. I never considered it a lesson in the seventh grade when my mother almost overdosed. Visiting my stepfather in jail never revealed anything for me. However, I was certain *Faces of Death*, a mondo-horror film, taught me about death.

As a kid, I watched films of every genre with my parents, but I mostly remember the horror movies we watched. In *The Anatomy of Genres*, author John Truby states the genre of horror revolves around the "sins of the past." I think about how I didn't reply to the last text my mother sent me. God commanded that children obey and honor their parents, and that there's no greater sin than ignoring your mother's text, especially if she's in another country asking you to send her money. That sounds to me like the premise of a horror film. The protagonist doesn't reply to his mother's text, and he's been haunted ever since. So, he writes about horror movies instead of the text he didn't send.

I remember the movie *Dr. Giggles* (1992). A psychopath who thinks he's a doctor returns to the town where his father was killed and begins killing people. I remember *Candyman* (1992). The vengeful ghost of an African American man who was brutally murdered for loving a white woman in the late nineteenth century appears when you say his name five times in the mirror. We watched these horror movies on VHS. I'd sit on the floor, my back to the bed. I'd face the television, the only light in the bedroom. My mother and stepfather would watch from the bed. I was always shocked at the abruptness of a loud noise and change of image on the screen during jump scares. I was shocked. I'd look up at my parents. I was worried they'd notice the fear in my eyes and recognize the shame I felt. But my parents weren't paying attention to me. They weren't even there. They were lost in the movie. Two young, beautiful faces in the TV glow, immersed in the horror.

The goal was to get students to write about themselves. They didn't ask, but I told them the word "essay" comes from the French "to try or attempt." I added that the word "ensayo" means both "essay" and "rehearsal" in Spanish. I mentioned Walter Benjamin's essay, the one he writes about being high off hashish somewhere in France. We listen to and read Nas's "OnThe goal of the class assignment was to get students to write about themselves. They didn't ask, but I told them the word "essay" comes from the French word *essai*, "to attempt or try." I added that the word "*ensayo*" means both "essay" and "rehearsal" in Spanish. I mentioned philosopher Walter Benjamin's 1927 essay, the one he writes about being high off hashish somewhere in France. We listen to and read Nas's "One Love." I'd forgotten that these students weren't adolescents at the turn of the century. They weren't teenage me in the early aughts.

The assignment was to write what they remember about yesterday. When they tell me they don't know what to write, I quote Baldwin: "When you're writing, you're trying to find out something which you don't know...."

Back when I was a high school teacher, Smart Boards weren't in every high school classroom. If there was a Smart Board that accessed YouTube, I played clips of James Baldwin interviews. Some schools blocked YouTube. The same YouTube students were able to connect to it with their cell phones and at home.

Videos of Baldwin strolling the streets got their attention. I showed a clip where Baldwin tells Dick Cavett: "Perhaps I don't think that this Republic is a summit of human civilization. Perhaps I don't want to become like Ronald Reagan or like the president of General Motors. Perhaps I have another sense of life which in fact my situation here has forced me to trust. And perhaps I know more about you and your institutions than you know about me. And perhaps I have a judgment on them. Perhaps I don't want what you think I want. Perhaps there is something that I can give you...."

For most of the teenagers I served, there's no going from video to reading. They wanted to keep watching YouTube. Watching Baldwin. And I wanted to keep watching Baldwin too. I wanted to "bear witness," doom-scrolling the algorithm. Back-to-back images of everything everywhere. I could spend hours watching clips of Baldwin, pretending to research.

When my students complain they would rather keep watching Baldwin instead of reading, I complain social media is destroying their attention span. I admit I can barely read these days. The older I get the harder it is to read Baldwin or anything else. It's easier when I read aloud or read while listening to the audiobook at the same time. Reading has always been hard for me, but these days it feels impossible. Words used to conjure their literal meaning; now they trigger a mess of connotations.

~

Currently, I'm working my last summer for an afterschool program in Harlem. After leaving the Department of Education, I began working for a nonprofit that provides 24/7 holistic support for Black and Latinx youth. This is my last summer because after four years with the organization, I've been having flashbacks. Suddenly, it's not a sixteen-year-old

Black girl from the Bronx I'm talking with, but my teenage mother. Being fully present across the teenagers I serve transports me to the past that's stored inside me. So, I have to pretend it's not my mother talking to me about why she snuck out of the workshop to make a TikTok dance video in the bathroom. I have to fake that it's not my stepfather and that it's a fifteen-year-old Dominican boy who recently arrived from Capotillo, Santo Domingo.

One warm winter, my cofacilitator and I were at Riverbank Park with our group of teens. They gradually joined us, as they were coming from high schools throughout New York City. One teenage girl sat on a bench across from my cofacilitator and me. The teen played with fries and a cheeseburger. She said the fries tasted like fridge. We were talking about alternatives to prisons when she reminded us her father did a ten-year bid. We knew this, but didn't know why. Without warning, while talking about Kalief Browder over soggy fries, she tells us her father shot the man who molested her.

This is the evil Baldwin said *The Exorcist* failed to portray. My cofacilitator and I continued to listen to the teen. She was matter of fact about her history. At some point, the teen became bored with us and got up to show her cell phone to another teenager. My cofacilitator and I looked at each other, anticipating our end-of-day debrief.

As this teen spoke about her father, she became my mother. She was my mother's age when she gave birth to me. I don't know what my mother went through as a child.

~

The actor Heath Ledger's autopsy and toxicology report concluded he died, "as the result of acute intoxication by the combined effects of oxycodone, hydrocodone, diazepam, temazepam, alprazolam, and doxylamine." I'm no expert, but I can't help but think it was benzodiazepines that got him. It depresses the nervous system, slowing your breathing and bringing you closer to the big sleep.

When I think of Heath Ledger, I don't think about his role as the Joker and then his tragic death as most people do. I think about how the actor was found with a movie script. According to director Stephen Gaghan, Ledger was supposed to star in the adaptation of Malcolm Gladwell's *Blink: The Power of Thinking Without Thinking*. The book is about the science of snap judgments and first impressions. Supposedly, the director Stephen Gaghan was obsessed with the chapter on emotions, which delves into how some people are good at immediately knowing what people are feeling or thinking. I had this ability with my mother when I was a kid, but the older I got, things changed. And I don't know if it's that I lost the gift or if she herself lost the ability to know what she was feeling or thinking with age.

I found spiritual teacher Osho's book, *Fear: Understanding and Accepting the Insecurities of Life*—the Spanish version—in my mother's bag when I searched her apartment in Cali, Colombia, after her death. I still haven't opened it. I also have a copy of Mitch Albom's *Tuesdays with Morrie*. My mother said the book reminded her of my relationship with my great-grandmother. I still haven't read it. Sometimes, I imagine dying not having read these books. Another text that followed my mother was *The Pill Book: The Illustrated Guide to the Most Prescribed Drugs in the United States*. My mother owned a copy when we lived on Riverside Drive by 181st Street. It was an older edition, tattered and worn. When I saw the book as a child it reminded me of the Bible. The mass market paperback 15th edition is 1,296 pages.

In Nice & Smooth's "Sometimes I Rhyme Slow," Smooth raps about a past lover. While the rapper was out on tour performing, this lover crashed his car. He finds out she was sniffing in his Mercedes-Benz. He raps: "Time went on I started noticin' weight loss / Then I had to ask her was she ridin' the white horse." For a long time, I thought the etymology of the slang "white horse" had to do with the Book of Revelations.

In the final book of the Bible, Death rides a pale horse as the fourth and final horseman of the apocalypse. From the King James version:

"And I looked, and behold a pale horse: and his name that sat on him was Death, and Hell followed with him. And power was given unto them over the fourth part of the earth, to kill with sword, and with hunger, and with death, and with the beasts of the earth."

In 2024, when I take the MTA subway, I feel like I'm in the Book of Revelations. I see bodies on the platform, and I can't tell if they're living or dead. Not that it matters to me because I'm more worried about my other fellow passengers. There are headlines of people getting pushed on the train tracks, so I'm ready to defend my life.

I'm writing this during a presidential election year and according to social media and mainstream news, my vote will determine whether or not we accelerate toward the end. On social media, I follow friends who are attacking people not posting about Israel's genocide against the Palestinian people. Silence in violence. Meanwhile, both warring parties in Sudan—the Rapid Support Forces and the Sudanese Armed Forces—have been accused of rape and gang rape. Just last year, the conflict in the eastern Democratic Republic of the Congo turned thirty. The election results have declared Nicolás Maduro the president of Venezuela. On social media, you're either an interventionist in support of the right and US Empire or a communist in support of dictatorship. Amid all this, President Joe Biden dropped out of the race, making Vice President Kamala Harris the democratic presidential nominee. Democrats and Republicans alike support and fund the genocide. The images of dead babies and dead children are no longer jump scares. Did I mention that Trump survived an assassination attempt?

It's August of 2024, and the last cohort of the students I taught within the Department of Education is in their early twenties. All the youth I taught are of voting age. I wonder if they're losing sleep over the US elections or Israel committing genocide against the people of Gaza. I imagine one of them telling me something about "the lesser of two evils." I wonder how many have reached a point Baldwin describes in "The Artist's Struggle for Integrity," where he says, "Most of us [white and black] have arrived at a point where we still believe and insist on and act on the principle, which is no longer valid, that this is such and such an optimum, that our choice is the lesser of two evils, and this is no longer true. Gonorrhea is not preferable to syphilis."

I'm glad they are no longer teenagers and I'm no longer their teacher because I don't want to contaminate them. I remember leaving the theater after having seen the documentary *Fahrenheit 9/11* (2004) feeling hope. My vote that year wasn't for the democrats or John Kerry, my vote was against Vice President Dick Cheney and Secretary of Defense Donald Rumsfeld. I was with my friend Hansel. He couldn't vote because of his immigration status. We both agreed this was a shame because every vote was a matter of life and death. Looking back on it now, I don't know how much of a difference it would have made if Senator John Kerry had become the US President. But we were kids back then who believed in democracy. Baldwin says it's only a matter of time before one is forced to "recognize that the major effort of our country until today is not to change a situation but to *seem* to have done it."

In his book, *Behold a Pale Horse,* Milton William "Bill" Cooper claims, "For many years the Secret Government has been importing drugs and selling them to the people, mainly the poor and minorities. Social welfare programs were put into place to create a dependent, nonworking element in our society. The government then began to remove the programs to force people into a criminal class that did not exist in the 1950s and 1960s."

While smoking weed with a friend in Amelia Gorman Park, a.k.a. Crackhead Park, in Washington Heights, I shared this passage. My friend didn't react how I thought he would. He asked me if I was going to vote for Trump. I said, "Hell no. I don't even know if I'm voting." My friend went on about how democracy was on the line and he used the phrase, "The End of Times." This friend had never voiced a political worldview, but he sounded like everyone on mainstream news and social media. This friend called Trump evil. He said many will die if he's elected. This friend of mine is a heroin dealer.

James Baldwin zoned out at his father's funeral. In "Notes of a Native Son," he wrote, "My mind was busily breaking out with a rash of disconnected impressions." Baldwin is nineteen years old. While watching over the children in attendance, he thinks of "Snatches of popular songs, indecent jokes, bits of books I had read, movie sequences, faces, voices, political issues," he says, "I thought I was going mad...."

In that moment, at his father's funeral, Baldwin had lost his own narrative thread. The part of the brain that gives life beginnings and endings. That thing between your ears that helps you determine the end. This is what happens to me when I try to meditate or when I try to fall asleep.

In *The White Album,* Joan Didion writes of the time she "began to doubt the premises of all the stories I had ever told myself, a common condition but one I found troubling." She shares a psychiatric report, the findings of a Thematic

Apperception Test. It described Didion's, "fundamentally pessimistic, fatalistic, and depressive view of the world around her." The first time I read this essay, I was in undergrad. Professor Yood at Lehman College gave me her marked up copy. Reading it then, I was shocked at how unique Didion's voice sounded. Reading it now, two months from forty, Didion's mental breakdown feels universal.

At this age, I read *The White Album* and *Notes of a Native Son* as two people navigating mental health during end times. Didion writes, "We live entirely, especially if we are writers, by the imposition of a narrative line upon disparate images, by the 'ideas' with which we have learned to freeze the shifting phantasmagoria which is our actual experience."

This gets me longing for one story to explain how the world got to be as it is now. How did *the fire this time*, at this present moment, come to be? How can so many of us suffer? How can we bear witness to a genocide without losing sleep? When I try figuring out how I sleep at night after experiencing hundreds of images showing dead Palestinian faces, I break night. However, it's not the faces of dead Palestinian babies I'm struggling with, but my lack of struggle after almost a year of dead faces.

~

From *Behold a Pale Horse*: "AIDS was introduced to the US population in 1978 when Hepatitis B vaccine trials were conducted by the Center for Disease Control in New York, San Francisco, and four other American Cities...Since large populations were to be decimated, the ruling elite decided to target the 'undesirable' elements of society. Specifically targeted were the black, Hispanic, and homosexual populations."

On many nights, this seems plausible even after reading about the writer. Milton William Cooper was an anti-Semite who claimed that President John F. Kennedy was assassinated because he was going to expose that extraterrestrials were taking over planet Earth.

Apache County deputies attempted to arrest Cooper at his Eagar, Arizona, home on November 6, 2001, for assault and endangerment. A gunfight ensued and Cooper was killed after shooting a deputy in the head.

Behold a Pale Horse is the ideal book for anyone who sees the end everywhere and meaning nowhere.

It seems to me the four horsemen have been galloping since this country's inception. One's seeing is not a curtain rising on a stage. One's seeing had nothing to do with the eyes, but reaching an age. At some point, the several jump scares you thought were one-offs become coincidences. Until one day, these jump scare coincidences become a pattern. You see them everywhere in the map of your life. The Four Horsemen have always been, your whole life has been an extended ending, it just knows you have the lens of times through which to see. It's not an apparition, but noticing the mundane.

And then, one day, my ten-year-old daughter asks, "Why did this happen?" Dead babies being dug out of rubble. I don't know what to tell my daughter or where to start. But I know it started long before October 7, 2023

~

In *Down at the Cross: Letter from a Region in My Mind*, Baldwin writes that at the age of fourteen, for him, "School began to reveal itself, therefore, as a child's game that one could not wine even though I no longer had any illusions about what an education could do for me; I had already encountered too many college-graduate handymen."

These teens know a high school diploma doesn't mean shit. If you're rich and you drop out, it doesn't matter. If you're poor and you graduate, it doesn't matter.

I tell them to at least finish high school. When they show any curiosity in higher education, I sell it. Tell them it's a different world, a safer world. I emphasize they should never-ever-ever-ever take out loans.

It's how I made it out, through a higher education. So, I project. Made it out of what, exactly? My block. Gone from my great-grandmother's apartment. Now my grandmother's apartment. I didn't really make out; instead, I moved. I moved from St. Nicholas Avenue overlooking the neon Riverside Drive Taxi Base sign. I moved west across Broadway to Haven Avenue near J. Hood Wright Park. I couldn't afford the peace and quiet on the other side of Broadway, so I moved again. Even with all my higher education, I couldn't afford west of Broadway Washington Heights.

I moved out of my great-grandmother's apartment, but the childhood lived within those walls remains. I tell students I took out loans. I tell them to get a high school diploma. I don't know what else to say.

How long have I misled teens? In my third year of teaching at a high school in Washington Heights, I was awarded Instructional Lead of the Year. The truth is, I got the award for my work with other adults, not for my work with students. Many of these kids were immigrants who lived or commuted to and spent most of their time in Washington Heights. The neighborhood is a portal. Six bridges. The I-95 runs through it. Drugs come in there, drugs are sold there, drugs are consumed there. And yet, there's no conversation with these students about drugs besides "don't use them." No conversation on the possibility that someone in that classroom might use drugs and or sell drugs. The only directive and expectation for those teens was: "Just say no."

~

"James Baldwin's biological father is said to have been a drug addict; his mother had to leave while Jimmy was still in utero," writes Harmony Holiday.

I also read this claim on several websites without any citations. This belief makes me feel less lonely. Reading about the opioid epidemic in the United States reminds me I'm not alone in death. This knowledge does nothing to my shame. Beth Macy opens *Raising Lazarus: Hope, Justice, and the Future of America's Overdose Crisis* with the etymology of stigma. "In ancient Rome, when tormentors branded an enslaved person with a hot iron, the scar left behind was called a *stigma*." In the Middle Ages, it meant the wounds the government left on Jesus's body. Shame and stigma were used interchangeably by the seventeenth century.

Macy writes: "It turns into a given, then, that stigmatized people are branded and judged as beyond redemption, as ruined. Drug-addicted people often react to stigma by excluding themselves from public life. They do this, in part, because drugs feel good when the actual world doesn't. Drugs help them forget, set aside, and numb their feelings of shame in a looping effect that exacerbates the very behaviors society initially reproached them for. In this way social

death can become literal death."

For a long time, I was ashamed of my mother. I was ashamed of my stepfather. This shame has nothing to do with either of them. It's about me. How *you* perceive me. *You* could be a stranger who is a user or a childhood friend whose own brother and cousin overdosed. No matter who *you* are.

My stepfather texted me saying it was an emergency. The emergency was money. On the phone, he told me he had just gotten out of rehab and needed money to get home. He asked if I could send money to his Chime account because he didn't have CashApp or Zelle. I downloaded the Chime app and created an account, but I couldn't send him the money. We spoke on the phone trying to find a way. I hit up my younger sister, asked if she had a Chime account. She said he was only going to use it on drugs. I told her I already knew that.

My stepfather said he needed the money to get to his mother's place in Jersey City. So, I told him I could order him a Lyft to his mother's address. I checked in with my sister to make sure the address he gave me was his mother's address. The address my stepfather gave me was in fact his mother's address. When I tell this story to childhood friends, survivors of the drug game, I make sure to not sound too serious, so it sounds like a punchline and not an ending. These friends are the sons and daughters of drug pushers and consumers, some who have overdosed. They've suffered enough to find humor in substance abuse. The Lyft app shows a little car following a purple line that ends at my stepfather's mother's home. And then something happens to the purple line. The purple line moves, ending at a different location. The little car makes a right turn. The final destination is no longer my stepfather's mother's home.

At this part of the story, I typically say, "When I saw that the address changed from his mom's crib to a Martin Luther King Drive, I knew we was in trouble."

It always hits—that part always gets laughs.

After this, I mastered talking about my stepfather's substance abuse with childhood friends who know the details. We never speak about it openly. We laugh. I make my sister, Mati, laugh. I make Alexo laugh. I almost make Abe laugh. Only Abe hesitates before he smiles.

When the Lyft driver arrives to pick up my stepfather I text: "He's in front of the Dunkin'. Let me know when you're home."

He replies: "I'm in the cab, answer."

I text back: Let's talk this weekend ███████ . This is throwing me off.

He: Don't worry, thanks for the ride.

Me: I love you ███████ . Be easy on your moms.

He: Nah fuck that. I always try to be there for everyone but when I ask for one thing everybody wants to find reasons not to help me.

Me: Say less ██████ .

~

Maybe my obsession with getting teenagers to self-reflect was the projection of my own suppressed needs. Maybe my caginess with that one therapist was a form of protecting my inner child. If set free, who would I be? Except a forty-year-old man responsible for himself and his daughter.

I am attached to the fifth grader who wrote the story of a boy whose parents were secretly vampires. My handwriting has always been shit. In elementary school, penmanship—neatness and few eraser marks—guaranteed your work a place on the bulletin board. At ten, I understood that all teachers valued presentation and the shape of the bottle over the liquid inside. But something changed in October 1994.

That fall, Ms. Arroyo, my fifth-grade teacher, asked that I revise my Halloween short story. Her only edit was the ending. The original ended with an M. Night Shyamalan twist where the parents weren't actually vampires, they were just playing a prank on the narrator. Ms. Arroyo asked me to rewrite it. She emphasized the word "neat" in her request. I rewrote it and she asked that I rewrite it again. I rewrote it a second time and she examined the handwritten story again. I know she wanted me to rewrite it, but she accepted the story that third time. On the bulletin board, my story stood out at a glance because of the handwriting. The unsteady lines that made letters revealed my uncertainty. Suspicion at my very certainty of thought. Since the fifth grade, I've been convinced I am a writer.

It wasn't until 2020, the year most of the world shut down because of the pandemic, that I realized most people read to find answers that already reside inside of them. This was the same year I left the Department of Education. That year, I published *On the Tip of Your Mother's Tongue.* I've always been a reader. But I'd taken for granted that other readers don't look for questions in their reading, but answers. Chehkov comes to mind.

Folks who read the *On the Tip of My Mother's Tongue* want answers about my mother. Their questions have as much to do with their curiosity as it does with their own relationship with their mothers. In my answers, I omit my experience and relationship with my mother. My writing did little to help me understand that. In *The White Album,* Didion admits, "writing has not yet helped me to see what it means."

I was working as a data entry specialist for a nonprofit in Queens when I found out my great-grandmother died. Days earlier, in the Dominican Republic, she had told me, on her deathbed, "cuida esa loca." When I got the news of my great-grandmother's death, I left work early and walked from Queens to Manhattan, only stopping at a used bookstore where I bought one of the volumes of George Orwell's diary.

I called my mother, who was working as a home attendant. She yelled at me, angry that I'd called her while she was in the middle of work. She hung up on me. At some point during my walk from Queens to Manhattan, my uncle called.

He was angry with me because I hadn't informed him of my great-grandmother's death. She'd died in the middle of the night, hours before his flight to the Dominican Republic.

Days later, my mother asked me to tell my little sister, Melo, about our great-grandmother's death. We were at my mother's apartment on University Avenue in the Bronx. I sat next to Melo. My mother was there. Mati, my other sister, was there. My stepfather was there. And maybe my uncle. I can't recall exactly. They all watched me tell my youngest sister that her great-grandmother had passed away. She began crying. I hugged her.

It was Mati, who told me about my mother's death four years later. Mati told me about my stepfather's death—her father—eight years later. It was me who told my grandmother about my stepfather's death. By the time of my stepfather's death, I had experienced so much death, I had no doubts about the news. I was certain he was gone.

~

Reading about the United States in the 1950s and 1960s in 2004 reminds me that the Book of Revelations is not a final act, but the perpetual present. "God gave Noah the rainbow sign, no more water, the fire next time!" The rainbow, the flooding, and the fire is happening now as I transcribe onto a laptop, deciphering the handwriting on my notepad.

I read in the words "The Fire Next Time," the promise that it can always get worse. On some nights, I find this is comforting.

~

In Baldwin's essay "The Artist's Struggle for Integrity," he writes: "You must understand that your pain is trivial except insofar as you can use it to connect with other people's pain; and insofar as you can do that with your pain, you can be released from it, and then hopefully it works the other way around too; insofar as I can tell you what it is to suffer, perhaps I can help you to suffer less." He goes on to say, "One is attempting to save an entire country, and that means an entire civilization, and the price for that is high. The price is to understand oneself." There's a difference between self-reflection and licking each other's wounds in community.

Essayist and poet June Jordan writes in *Some of Us Did Not Die*, "I am saying that the ultimate connection cannot be the enemy. The ultimate connection must be the need that we find between us. It is not only who you are, in other words, but what we can do for each other that will determine the connection." I believe the ultimate connection is our children. Like Baldwin said, "The price...is to recognize that most of us, white and black, have arrived at a point where we do not know what to tell our children. How do you talk about breaking news with a ten-year-old? Or a seventy-six-year-old for that matter? How does one reflect without being consumed by all the suffering in the world?" They are all our children.

~

Presidential election years in the United States feel like the Book of Revelations. Civilization and democracy are on the line. Vice President Kamala Harris, a former prosecutor, is the Democratic nominee. Donald Trump, the former president, a right-wing insurrectionist, is the Republican nominee. The Democratic National Convention takes place in Chicago this year. I imagine breaking news, local, national and international; the worst-case scenario; living in the fire next time that's to come. I can imagine either Harris or Trump as president. I imagine a president, an amorphous face perpetually changing, adapting its phenotype and social identity. No matter the face, I don't feel safe.

I am certain we will always be confronted with hurting teenage faces, the faces of young people who will nevertheless survive the never-ending breaking news. I don't know what we are supposed to tell our teenagers. I don't know what we are supposed to teach them. I do know we have to keep them hopeful. I do know they need hope. We all need hope. And I don't mean the feeling that comes from voting. I'm talking about the kind of hope that comes with speaking with your children like they deserve to know the truth. Once you tell them the truth, you've done your part. There's hope in knowing that at least one person in the world has not tried to deceive them. I believe in earned hope.

In the documentary *Take This Hammer* (1963), Baldwin speaks to residents and activists of Black neighborhoods in San Francisco. A teenager tells him there will never be a Black president explaining, "We can't get jobs, how we going to be president?" Baldwin replies, "It's not important really, you know, whether or not there is a Negro president, I mean in *that* way. What's important is that you should realize that you can become the president. There's nothing anybody can do that you can't do...."

Our teenagers in general, New York City Black boys in particular, should feel like they can be. And then one day, they'll grow out of myths and aspire to be something greater than president or drug dealer.

In order to create a world where humanity can exist and cope no matter who is elected president, we have to talk and listen to our teenagers as if they have the World Wide Web in their pockets. They are also witnesses testifying on the stand. We can't pretend they don't know what is happening in their homes and in the world. We can't silence them because we fear what they'll say and how they'll say it. We can't let the fear of being called out for our complicity as adults. We have to expose them to other ways of thinking and being. Sometimes that means letting them be. Ways of existing in the world, which believes in the best of human nature and accepts the fact that safety is not certain. No prison-industrial complex, no police presence, no surveillance and no criminalization of drug consumption will make teenagers and children safer.

The truth is that adults do not know the way. So, as adults, all we can do is talk about the world with teens as it is and not as we pretend it to be. There always comes a point in the lives of adults with teenagers in their life, when a subject comes up and adults must negotiate whether they should encourage the teen to act as someone in the world as the world should be or act in the world as it is. Does the adult tell them to turn the other cheek or reveal to them that sometimes all it takes is turning the other cheek once for the world to take a swivel out your neck. Does the adult tell the teenager "Just say no" to drugs without explaining what happens or what to do when other teenagers around them are using drugs? Does the adult ever consider that their own teenager might experiment with drugs? At this moment, does the parent realize that omission does not protect, but postpones betrayal? When does the parent reveal the truth to their teenager?

Adolescence is the Book of Revelations. The world you thought you knew is gradually ending with each change in your body and each mask falling off the faces of those adults in your family. There is always a point in one's life as a teenager when one realizes the adults don't know what they're doing. There's a before and after in the story you tell yourself about your mother, your father, and other adults in your life.

This made you angry because in essence, they lied and omitted the truth about themselves. And these truths about them allowed them to cast judgment and punish you like some diva God throwing a tantrum.

How do we speak to our teenagers without a mask? We can't hide our face from teenagers forever. Sooner or later, they will be adults. Sooner or later, we will die and our masks will be taken off for us. It's heartbreaking that so many famous people's lives have been reduced to the way they died. Famous people and people we know. When an autopsy reveals the death was due to an overdose, the story of the person's life becomes something else in the mind of those who never knew them. Autopsy derives from the Greek autopsia, meaning "seeing with one's own eyes."

There is no one moment when the real adult world is revealed to our teenagers. Our teenagers won't complete a transformation process that will equip them with processing adult truths. They are exposed to drugs at school, their neighborhoods, and online. Preparing them for a world with mood-altering substances a.k.a. drugs by telling them to resist and refuse is setting them up for failure.

In *The Harm Reduction Gap: Helping Individuals Left Behind by Conventional Drug Prevention and Abstinence-only Addiction Treatment*, author and harm reductionist Sheila P. Vakharia goes over the failure of the "Just Say No" drug prevention campaign and abstinence-only treatment. In the book, she referenced a 2021 survey that showed that

"Seventy percent of the US population over the age of twelve had used alcohol, a tobacco or nicotine product, or an illegal drug in the past year. And nearly sixty percent of people in the nation, over one hundred million people, had used one of these substances in the past month."

A lot of people are using drugs for many different reasons, and yet there's no honest conversation taking place. There are spaces that focus on formal addiction treatment where people can get substance-related support, but these spaces are for folks with addictions or diagnosable substance use disorders. Some are Overdose Prevention Centers (OPCs). These centers provide a place where people can safely use previously obtained drugs under the

supervision of trained staff. What happens with those who consume drugs or alcohol in social settings, sporadic bingers, or experimenters? Our focus has been on preventing drug use and treating those addicted. What about everyone else who uses drugs?

According to Dr. Vakharia, "People can live safe and fulfilling lives in a world with drugs, if armed with proper tools and education...."

~

Mati called me to tell me about my mother's death. She called me to tell me about my stepfather's death. I commend my sister because even through our parents' addictions and mental health issues, she stuck by their side and was welcoming whenever they returned. I took breaks from my mother and stepfather. To be frank, there were many, many months—if not years—where I didn't speak to them. I wonder if they'd be alive if they had had an Opioid Prevention Center in their lives. I wonder how the last text messages between us would have gone if I didn't feel shame, guilt, and anger. Now, I know they wanted to feel normal. Getting high is about not sinking into the past. Anger at someone else getting high is about control. I was angry I couldn't stop them from getting high. I was angry that I couldn't protect them from death. And yet that didn't mean I should protect myself from being hurt by pretending they didn't exist. Before their deaths, I had deleted them from my life, because it was too difficult to confront and embrace them for who they were.

There were parts of myself I contained in what I wrote. I wrote in the second person to separate myself from myself and many people in my life. I wrote with so many silences because I didn't want to hear it. In "The Creative Process," Baldwin writes, "We are responsible for our actions, but we rarely understand them...if we understood ourselves better, we would damage ourselves less."

~

My daughter is almost a teenager. At my daughter's last doctor's visit, I barely spoke. She explained her daily routine, her diet, and goals next school year. She spoke clearly about her body and school life. At some point, the doctor asked that if at any moment she would feel more comfortable being with a woman doctor, she should let me or her mom know.

At that moment, I felt something I felt once before. When my great-grandmother on her deathbed told me, "Take care of that crazy woman." I felt it then. When my stepfather sent me a text that even though he tries to be there for others, they always find reasons not to help when he asks for help. I felt it then. My ten-year-old daughter speaking for herself at the doctor's office felt like the foreshadowing of an inevitable ending.

An impending meeting with death. There is no doubt that I will die and she will mourn. But that's not the death I'm concerned with—at least not right now. I'm talking about her becoming a teenager and seeing the face behind my mask. And she will be certain in what she now only suspects. The father she sees me as will die. My daughter will learn I *am* the wizard from the *The Wizard of Oz* (1939). A movie we've watched several times. The last time we watched it, she was interested in Dorothy. Not Dorothy, but Judy Garland. She asked if

Dorothy was still alive. I know in the near future, she'll learn either from me or the world that the teenage Garland was forced to take stimulants to keep her working long hours. By 1968, Garland was taking Valium, Ritalin, and Thorazine. Supposedly, she was taking as much as forty Ritalin pills every day. Whether I reveal the facts about the teenage Judy Garland or omit what happened behind the scenes, my daughter will discover the truth.

I'll be past forty and my daughter will be a teenager. She'll have many questions about me, about her mother, my mother, her grandmother, and great-grandmother. I will tell her what I know. I will read James Baldwin with her without dismissing what she sees between the words. I will listen how I listened to her at the doctor's office. And pay attention. My goal is to give her my attention—in other words, love. We will watch R-rated movies together. We will talk about death without divorcing it from life.

I will be an honest father and a good writer.

Acknowledgments

Acknowledgement is made to the following journals where versions of these stories have appeared:

The Poetry Project: "Buying Cocaine"
Post [Blank] Magazine: "Almost All About Your Mother"
Kweli Journal: "Without a Big One"
433 : "Bachata"
Mosaic Literary Magazine: "On Screens"

~

Thank you, Josh Dale, for always being down to do something different and taking risks for the sake of making readers out of non-readers. Thank you Anna Suarez and the crew at Thirty West.

Thank you: BMCC, Sayida Self, Maria Kromidas, Jim Tolan, Page Delano, Lehman College: Terrence Cheng, Salita Bryant, Tyler T. Schmidt, The New School, Dale Peck, Robert Antoni, the tHe beRnACulaR kReW, The Brotherhood Sister Sol, Jason Warwin, Cidra Sebastian, Khary Lazzare White, Ummi Modeste, Dominican Writers, Angy Abreu, Mariela Regalado, Kweli Journal, and Laura Pegram.

Thank you to Robert Carlos Garcia for "listening" to "On Screens" in conversation before helping me develop the essay. Thank you, Danny Vasquez, for always reading anything and everything I send his way. Thank you, Alexo Batista, for being the best reader and reading for reading's sake and not because it's part of your "identity," like so many of us who read.

Thank you, Katherine, for seeing me. You're the best partner in every sense of the word. I love you.

Thank you, Amelie, for all your help and feedback. Your courage and work ethic are inspiring. Thank you, Mati, for parenting our parents until the end. Your grace has taught me a lot.

About The Author

JP Infante is the author of *On the Tip of Your Mother's Tongue* and *Aquí y Allá: un retrato de la comunidad Dominicana en Washington Heights*. He is the winner of The PEN America Robert J. Dau Short Story Prize and Thirty West's Wavelengths Chapbook contest. His writing has appeared in *Kweli*, *The Poetry Project*, and elsewhere. He has been awarded scholarships and fellowships from the NY State Writers Institute, PEN America, and The Center for Fiction. He holds an MFA from The New School. Currently, he's an organizer and facilitator for the Liberation Program at the Brotherhood-Sister Sol, a non-profit in Harlem that has served Black and Latinx youth with wrap-around services for almost 30 years.

About the Publisher

Escape the Mundane

Est. 2015

Follow us on:

Scan the QR code to visit.

www.thirtywestph.com

EN LA PUNTA DE LA LENGUA DE TU MADRE

OBRAS SELECCIONADAS

JP INFANTE

Thirty West
Publishing
❦❦
10 YEARS
2015-2025

Amberlyn aka Mati

"Mi forma normal de ser es realmente apoyar, animar, elogiar, alimentar y cuidar a todos los que entran en mi hogar. Pero si, a causa de la opresión, la discriminación, el abuso, la falta de respeto, pierdo el equilibrio que necesito para cumplir esta función—que es muy innata—entonces no puedo ser el ser que estoy aquí para ser. Y cuando piensas en todas las mujeres, en todas las madres del mundo que no solo no reciben apoyo, sino que activamente están siendo pisoteadas, no es ningún misterio que el mundo esté en el estado en el que está."

—Alice Walker

TABLA DE CONTENIDO

En la Punta de la Lengua de Tu Madre

CORDÓN UMBILICAL

1.

Salías corriendo de la escuela donde ella te esperaba. La miraste a la cara y oliste alcohol en su aliento.

Al cruzar la calle le hablaste del Profesor Castro y de cómo amenazó con darle una pela a cualquier niño que se peleara en la clase.

Ella te tomó de la mano y frunció el ceño "Yo lo pico" dijo. El chirrido de unos neumáticos paralizó todo. El carro casi te atropella. Ella te haló del hombro y gritó: ¡La luz 'ta amarilla!

El conductor se sacudió en el carro, agarrándose del volante.

Ella te soltó el hombro cuando llegaste a la acera. El apretón. Tu moratón. No le tenías miedo al conductor, ni al profesor Castro, sino que temías por ellos.

2.

Antes de salir de Rikers tomaste tus pertenencias del armario. La guagua estaba llena de madres, hermanas, hijas, niños pequeños y el calentón del verano.

Una persona molestaba a otra dizque por un asiento que le pertenecía a otra persona.

La mujer corpulenta le gritó a tu madre. Tu madre te lanzó a tu hermanita de un mes y se enfrentó cara a cara con la mujer corpulenta, gritándole mucho más fuerte.

El conductor de la guagua le suplicaba a las mujeres, mientras forcejeaba con el timón.

Pensaste que el conductor llevaría a tu madre de regreso a la cárcel por estar peleando, pero era solamente miedo.

No le temías a la cárcel ni a la mujer corpulenta.

Temías dejar caer a tu hermanita.

3.

Esto fue antes de tu hermana, antes de muchas otras cosas. Vivías en un apartamento con una mujer y su hijo pequeño. Los ratones dormían debajo de una montaña de juguetes en la sala.

Una cola como de gusano se deslizaba entre figurines de acción, cabello de muñecas, y animales de peluche.

No recuerdas ni la cocina, ni el baño, o la mujer que le alquilaba a tu madre.

Recuerdas tu pequeño dormitorio y las paredes azules. Había una ventana rota y un radiador frío junto a la cama doble.

Durante toda la noche temblabas en sus brazos. Por la mañana te ponías el gorro, el abrigo y los guantes para ir a la escuela y, aun así, sentías un friito colarse por las grietas en la ventana. No sabías si lo que sentías era miedo o frío, o si existía alguna diferencia.

COMPRANDO COCAÍNA

1.

Lleva contigo a un amigo afrolatino o negro.

No confundas a tus amigos españoles con tus amigos que hablan español. Tu proveedor nunca ha estado en España y fingirá que no sabe ni un chin de inglés si se le acercan dos tipos blancos.

Tu proveedor piensa que blanco es blanco al igual tú crees que el negro es negro. Tu proveedor nunca te cobrará de más si te acompaña una persona de color.

2.

Embuste. No se trata de ti. Tu proveedor te cobrará de más no porque seas blanco, sino porque puedes.

Este barrio no es tan diferente a ese resort al que fuiste en el Caribe. Tu proveedor es más americano de lo que crees. Es un aspirante a capitalista como esos trabajadores hoteleros del tercer mundo.

Plátanos con Salami.

Brugal con Coca-Cola.

La cosita húmeda y jugosa, de color morado celeste, de esa mujer tan negra como el carbón.

Allá te cobraron de más. Aquí también lo harán.

3.

Concéntrate en el perico.

Cuando salgas del puente George Washington estarás en la calle 178 y Fort Washington junto a la terminal de guaguas. Parecerá la Naciones Unidas. Verás tecatos blancos, marrones, y negros de todas partes del mundo. Esto no es *Bright Lights, Big City* (Luces de neón). Esto es el verdadero cosmopolitismo.

El barrio está compuesto por norteamericanos, incluyendo indocumentados respetuosos de la leyes.

Olvídalos.

4.

Maneja por la calle 178 y gira a la izquierda en la Avenida Wadsworth. Ignora el merengón que sale por las ventanas y el reggaeton que dejan atrás los carros que pasan a toda marcha. Ignora a los tigueres en sus sillas de plástico frente a los

edificios, bebiendo y celebrando Dios sabe qué vaina en la Avenida Saint Nicholas.

Tira tu CD de 50 Cent por la ventana del carro. Irónicamente, escuchar un CD de 50 Cent, que has comprado, prueba tu blancura y no lo oculta.

5.

Sé tú mismo. Sé blanco. No seas como los maleantes de las esquinas. No te ayudará en nada. La verdad es que el maleanteo ama la blancura más de lo que tú o ellos podrían llegar a entender.

Lee *Black Skin, White Masks* (Piel negra, máscaras blancas) de Frantz Fanon o el resumen de los capítulos de Wilhelm Von Schadow en la *Liberator Magazine*.

6.

Evita caminar por la iglesia. Si pasas a pie, los feligreses se darán cuenta que olvidaste hacer la señal de la cruz. Además, sabrán que no estuviste en la misa el domingo pasado. Para ellos se trata de comunidad y caridad y tú eres un extraño que todavía no ha donado.

7.

Mientras buscas parqueo descubrirás que una universidad, para un grupo específico de personas, está a una cuadra de distancia de tu concesionario. Parquea frente a la secundaria George Washington. La tasa de deserción escolar es tan alta como tan bajo el dinero del impuesto a la propiedad que va a la escuela.

8.

No te sorprendas al ver personas con la puedas identificarte. La renta está más cara que nunca, por eso muchos nos estamos mudando. La renta es barata: Considera mudarte a esa zona.

9.

El alcalde Giuliani limpió la ciudad, pero sus manos no están limpias. Sus soldados usaron un desatascador en un inmigrante haitiano mientras protegían y servían. Afortunadamente, tu estás lejos de esa piel oscura haitiana así que estás a salvo.

10.

No hables mal del último jodedor que te vendió la harina que ahora te anestesia la lengua. La mayoría de estos distribuidores se han tratado entre sí, y si todavía no lo han hecho lo harán. Algunos de ellos son más industriosos que tú, invierten en lavanderías hasta que sus secadoras paren de girar, ya el dinero estará limpio, y la lavandería pasará a ser un negocio local como lavandería real. La mayoría de estos proveedores ya están presis. Algunos de estos bloques son trampas, más pequeños que pequeñas ciudades. Lee a *Winesberg, Ohio* de Sherwood Anderson, y *Dublineses* de James Joyce.

11.

Cuando llegues al bloque de tu distribuidor evita a Terrence. Él tiene más o menos tu edad. Se da cuenta que eres blanco y no de Europa del Este y él te lo echará en cara. El leyó *Un lugar pequeño* de Jamaica Kincaid y todavía está enojado. Él está en esa prestigiosa escuela que no te aceptó a pesar de que los dos tenían notas idénticas. Tú pondrás los ojos en blanco y culparás a la Acción afirmativa.

Terrence soltará un chuipi y contrarrestará con Admisión de legado.

12.

Que ni se te ocurra sonreírle a Josefina. Ella estará esperando por su papá frente al edificio de tu proveedor. El papá de Josefina, el taxista, no hace otra cosa que no sea trabajar, leer el periódico, y llevar a su hija de un lado a otro. El sólo sabe de béisbol. Nunca ha jugado al golf y cree que Tiger Woods es un lugar al norte en el estado de Nueva York, y sin embargo es dueño de un palo de golf hierro cuatro. Aléjate de su hija. El es vieja escuela y fue oprimido en los días que estaba de moda la opresión descarada. Él te va a entrar a ramplimazo con su palo de golf como si la Avenida St. Nicholas fuera ese charco de río que divide la isla Hispaniola, y hubieras pronunciado una palabra en Español de la manera incorrecta. Lee *Cosecha de huesos*, de Edwidge Danticat.

13.

Encontrarás al proveedor esperándote en el tercer piso. Cuando le digas que yo te mandé, el sacará el perico. No le digas de dónde y cómo me conoces ni le preguntes a él de dónde y cómo me conoce. Él cuenta el dinero una y otra vez y te llenas de ansiedad. Temes que te robe como lo hizo tu último proveedor la última vez que fuiste al barrio a capear. Él no estará en habladera. No te dirá que le ha facilitado

producto a mi mamá a mis espaldas, pero esta historia no se trata de eso.

Cuando finalmente te dé el producto te sentirás aliviado, y le preguntarás a modo de broma cuánto es el corte que lleva.

El traficante te recordará que nada es puro.

CASI TODO SOBRE TU MADRE

Tenías siete u ocho años la primera vez que cuestionaste la cordura de tu madre. Antes de entrar en una oficina de Administración de Recursos Humanos en Washington Heights, te dijo: "Si preguntan, dile que 'toy loca'. Al sol de hoy, no estás seguro de si estaba bromeando.

Esto fue en los tiempos anteriores a las tarjetas EBT. Ustedes parecían hermanos, una hermana mayor con su hermanito, solicitando cupones de alimentos. La trabajadora de la HRA era una mujer negra alta y delgada con lentes. Tu madre pensaba que para obtener elegibilidad para los cupones de alimentos los solicitantes tenían que estar lo—incluso a esa edad—que a los padres que estaban locos les quitaban los hijos.

Mientras la trabajadora de la HRA interrogaba a tu madre, esperabas a que te preguntaran por su salud mental.

Pensaste mucho en la pregunta. Ahora que escribes esto, te preguntas si realmente conociste a tu mamá. La recuerdas durmiendo mucho. Escuchaba música hasta altas horas de la

noche causando discusiones con los vecinos. Ella se quejaba de las facturas y aun así te compraba cualquier juguete que le pedías. Tu madre respondía a las preguntas de la trabajadora de la HRA mientras tú esperabas a que te preguntara: "¿Está loca tu mamá?". Nunca te lo preguntaron. Tal vez porque la cordura no era un requisito para los cupones de alimentos o porque la respuesta era obvia.

Las mujeres de tu familia: bisabuela, abuela, y madre guardan silencio sobre su pasado y le dicen poco a los hombres de la familia: tu tío materno y tú.

Sin embargo, cuando están dolidas y enfadadas se recuerdan el dolor que se han causado mutuamente. Las mujeres de tu familia siempre han sido un misterio para los hombres de tu familia.

Estas mujeres son conocidas, pero sólo entre ellas.

Durante una discusión entre tu madre y tu abuela, te enteraste de que tu madre había sido internada en una sala de psiquiatría del Columbia Presbyterian a los 14 años. No recuerdas de qué trataba la discusión, excepto que tu mamá juró que nunca perdonaría a su madre por obligarla a ingresar en un lugar para locos.

Nunca pensaste que tu mamá estaba loca no porque era tu mamá, sino porque cada vez que decía estarlo o actuaba como si lo estuviera siempre había algún motivo oculto. Una vez se hizo la loca para conseguir un apartamento nuevo.

Cuando eras adolescente, tu bisabuela y tú fueron a visitar a tu madre a su apartamento en el Bronx. Ella odiaba el

apartamento e intentaba mudarse debido el mal mantenimiento y a la violencia del barrio. Cuando llegamos al edificio los Vecinos nos dijeron que mi mamá estaba en el hospital tras incendiarse su apartamento.

En el hospital te dijeron que tu mamá estaba internada en el área psiquiátrica porque sospechaban que ella había provocado el fuego. Tu bisabuela y tú estaban preocupados hasta que viste a tu mamá. Se había hecho amiga de los guardias de seguridad, doctores y pacientes de la unidad. Te presentó a todos. El contraste entre la energía de tu madre y el letargo y la dificultad en el habla de los otros pacientes te convenció de que no estaba loca.

Después de algunos trámites tu bisabuela abuela firmó su salida.

De camino a casa en el taxi dijo, "Fue chiquito el incendio. Yo voy a buscar un mejor sitio."

Tú preguntaste: "¿Por qué la gente allá era tan lenta?"

"Las pastillas", dijo ella, "Yo hacía que me las tragaba".

Tu madre tuvo razón. Ella consiguió un nuevo apartamento después del fuego.

El verano antes de cumplir tus 28 años visitaste a tu mamá en un pabellón psiquiátrico del Hospital Lebanon de Queens. Esta vez ella no estaba intentando conseguir dinero de algún programa social, o un apartamento, o la simpatía de la familia. Ella se quejó de que su ex, un capo traficante de drogas tenía gente que la llamaba por teléfono bromeando y siguiéndola a todos lados. En ese momento no estabas seguro de si ella

estaba actuando como una loca.

Al final no importaba. Se había encasillado a sí misma. Tu madre seguía asumiendo el mismo papel.

La unidad de psiquiatría estaba en un piso alto. La ventana de la sala de visitas mostraba un vasto paisaje del condado de Queens con el sol acostándose detrás del horizonte de Manhattan. Tu mamá sonrió y te dijo que quería quedarse dos días más para calmar sus nervios. Ella no estaba loca, sólo estresada. Mientras tu madre te hablaba un jovencito caminaba hacia ti. Al principio pensaste que era Dominicano como tú, pero te enteraste de que era egipcio y que estaba enamorado de tu mamá. Se presentó y te declaró su amor por tu mamá. Todos rieron.

Él dijo que que sólo tenía 21 años, pero que la trataría bien. Era encantador y buen mozo.

Tu madre le dijo que eras escritor, así que él empezó a contarte una idea que tenía para una novela. La historia trataría de sirenas obligadas a vivir en tierra y moverse en silla de ruedas.

Te preguntó si eras religioso y le dijiste, "A chepa católico".

Dijo que tu madre tendría que convertirse al Islam si se casaban. Todos rieron. Recitó unos versículos del Corán y ,aunque no lo entendías, apreciaste su musicalidad. Le preguntaste por su familia. Su madre había muerto recientemente después de batallar por años contra el cáncer. Dijo que su padre fue un buen hombre. Dijo que si se casaba

con tu madre sería un padrastro benévolo. Todos rieron.

Te aseguraron que tu mamá no estaba loca, y concluyeron que el joven egipcio intentaba sobrellevar la muerte de su madre, pero estaba cerca de perder el control por completo.

Mientras tu mamá te acompañaba a la salida susurró: "¿Qué tu cree'?".

"¿De qué?", dijiste.

"¿De casarme con él? Es de buena

Familia".

Miraste a tu mamá sin saber si estaba jugando.

Le preguntaste: "¿En serio?".

Ella te besó y te dijo: «Te llamó mañana».

De camino a casa en el tren 7, te diste cuenta de que tu madre quería tu bendición. Te dieron ganas de llorar. Hacía años que no llorabas. Cada vez que sientes el impulso, la voz de tu madre suena en tu cabeza, algo que te dijo una vez: "Cuando un hombre se faja a llorar por mí, le pierdo el respeto ahí mismo."

Te ves llorando en el reflejo de la ventanilla del vagón de tren, tu cara superpuesta sobre el horizonte de la ciudad de Nueva York bajo una noche sin estrellas. Tu reflejo te recuerda a tu mamá perdiendo el hilo de sus pensamientos con tu nombre en la punta de la lengua, como si en cualquier momento fuese a recordarlo.

SIN UN GRANDE

Has pensado en saltar.

Es una noche fría de invierno. Te sientas junto a Queeny en la escalera de incendios. Los autos en la autopista van y vienen como olas. Las luces del puente George Washington se reflejan en el río Hudson como el brillo de unos ojos vidriosos. El río es una bañera gigante sin un barco ni bote para salvar a alguien que pueda estar ahogándose.

Tu niñera, Nilda, dice que el suicidio es como matar a alguien y que, si sobrevives saltando por la escalera de incendios, la policía te arrestará por intento de asesinato. Si intentas suicidarte, tienes que planear superarlo porque el suicidio solo sentido si sobrevives. Nilda se rió cuando le dijiste que el intento es para llamar la atención de la gente. Se rió porque era verdad.

Sientes el viento frío. Observas los edificios al otro lado del río en New Jersey. Están muy separados, con mucho espacio entre ellos. Pero no hay espacio entre Queeny y tú porque ambos necesitan el calor.

Antes solían llamarte Minene, y antes de eso te llamaban

Chungo, aunque tu certificado de nacimiento dice otro nombre. Tu padrastro, que lleva tres meses lejos, estudiando en la escuela, te llama hijo. "Hijo, tráeme el control de la tele". "Hijo, escucha a tu madre". "Hijo, deja de hablar de tu corazón".

Tu padrastro puede dibujarte a ti y a tu pequeño corazón, a Queeny durmiendo en tus pies. Puede dibujar cualquier cosa y a cualquier persona. Él sabe todo sobre deportes, anime, videojuegos, cómics y juguetes. Es el hombre más fuerte que has conocido, y el único que te ha besado. Nunca te ha mentido. Cuando él empezó la escuela, sentiste ganas de llorar, pero no lo hiciste porque nunca lo habías visto llorar.

Mary te dio a luz. Te llama Mi nene o Ray y, a veces, por error, el nombre de tu padrastro. Mary no oye cuando la llamas mamá. Te llama Raymond cuando Queeny juega con sus zapatos o hace caca en la casa. Mary no quiere a Queeny como lo hace tu padrastro. Ella es más joven que las madres de todos tus amigos. Incluso se ve tan joven como tu niñera, pero sabes que Nilda es más joven porque es más feliz que tu madre.

A veces, duermes con Mary en el dormitorio y Te gusta frotar su pelo en tu nariz. A veces el olor a champú y cigarrillos te da sueño. A veces la mezcla de esos olores te mantiene despierto por la noche. Normalmente duermes en el sofá cama de la sala debido a tu enfermedad de vejiga. Últimamente te resulta difícil contener la orina por la noche.

Tu nuevo médico dice "*konnichiwa*" todo el tiempo. Dijo

que los niños que beben sodas se orinan en la cama, y Mary le creyó. No confías en este médico porque cuando le preguntaste si era chino, señaló un círculo rojo en el centro de un rectángulo blanco y dijo japonés. Luego le sonrió a Mary.

Una noche te quedaste dormido con Mary en el dormitorio, y sus ronquidos te despertaron alrededor de la medianoche. La televisión mostraba a unos ancianos hablando sobre la enfermedad de la vejiga. A la mañana siguiente, en la mesa de la cocina, le hablaste a Mary sobre la enfermedad de la vejiga. Ella estaba revolviendo el correo, con un cuchillo en mano. Se detuvo, miró el plato hondo que tenías frente a ti y dijo: *"Mentiroso"* antes de abrir un sobre rojo de un solo intento. Normalmente ella no habla español, así que no la entendiste. La forma en que Mary pronunció esa palabra la convirtió en una extraña.

Esa mañana te das cuenta de que el médico chino estaba coqueteando con ella. Tomas nota mental de avisarle a tu padrastro cuando llame desde la escuela. Solo ha llamado un par de veces desde que se fue, porque el teléfono del apartamento siempre está cortado y nunca hay minutos en el teléfono celular prepago de Mary.

Tu niñera, Nilda, te llama Ray Ray. Ella ama a Queeny. Nilda es más alta que Mary y tiene un culo grande. Cada vez que la abrazas, lo tocas y ella no dice nada. Nilda está enamorada de ti. No le dices que lo sabes porque ella tiene novio. Cada vez que Nilda te ve se ríe, pero no de ti, es solo que le da vergüenza estar enamorada de alguien de tu edad. Por la

noche, en la cama, te imaginas besando a Nilda y lamiéndole los labios.

Nilda es inteligente, hermosa y te lee cuentos con malas palabras, y palabras que no entiendes. Ella dice que eres maduro, que deberías dibujar tus propios dibujos en lugar de calcar. Un día, Nilda le dijo a su amiga, la de las tetas enormes, que serías un rompecorazones. Su amiga te preguntó: *"¿Serías mi novio?"* Tardaste un rato antes de responder porque no querías herir los sentimientos de Nilda. Dijiste:" *Depende"*y la amiga de Nilda se rió. Nilda apenas rió porque estaba celosa. Ese día supiste que tenías que compensarla. Entonces, cuando Nilda pidió algo de beber, le pusiste hielo en su Ginger Ale. Y cuando le diste el refresco, viste su rostro a través del vaso y Nilda parecía estar hecha de oro.

Nilda te recuerda a tu profesora de aula, la señora Vicioso, porque no es paternalista. Paternalista es una palabra que te enseñó Nilda. Cuando te pilló calcando los bocetos de tu padrastro, la señora Vicioso te dijo: *Puedes hacerlo mejor.*

Tu padrastro hizo un dibujo de Big Ralph, el dueño del supermercado en New Jersey que siempre está comiendo. Cada vez que Ralph te dice algo, lo termina con un: *¿Sabes a qué me refiero, Jellybean?* Ralph da miedo porque es más grande que ese gorila que viste en el zoológico. Su respiración suena como si acabara de subir las escaleras, incluso si ha estado sentado en una silla. A veces, mientras está de pie, se queda dormido. Parece que se va a caer de nalgas y nunca se va a levantar.

Nilda una vez llamó a Ralph como *Glue-Ton*. Dice que la palabra viene del latín en Grecia, y significa "tragar". Nilda dice que el latín es un idioma que está muerto porque se mató a sí mismo o alguien lo mató. No estás seguro de cómo llegaron los latinos a Grecia, pero la Sra. Vicioso dice que viven en todo el mundo gracias a España. Sabes que la palabra significa más que "tragar." Tiene que ver con alguien que no puede tener suficiente de algo, pero no puedes recordar lo que dijo Nilda.

Antes de que tu padrastro se fuera a la escuela, Ralph solía traer, bolsas de compras llenas de comida de su supermercado. El refrigerador ha estado vacío desde entonces y no has visto a Ralph. Has visto al amigo secreto de Nilda, Gregorio. Casi te olvidas de él porque Nilda dijo que no le dijeras a nadie que él vienía. No te gusta Gregorio porque cuando vino de visita solo le prestó atención a Nilda. Fuiste a calcar los dibujos de tu padrastro y te quedaste dormido en el sofá.

~

Hoy te despiertas con olor a orina y alcohol. No del tipo que te frotó el *wannabe* médico chino-japonés, sino al que huele Mary. ¿Te has hecho pipí? Sientes tu ropa interior. Quítatela. *El Superman* desteñido parece normal. Sécate. Te

pones la ropa para ir a la escuela. Mary no está despierta para hacerte duchar.

Hoy es diferente: no recorrerás el largo camino por la monótona Riverside Drive, ni subirás por una colina hasta Fort Washington Avenue. Hoy tomarás el atajo con tu mejor amigo, Frankie, aunque tu padrastro te ha dicho que no tomes el camino corto sin él.

Frankie te llama Ray Ray como al resto de tus compañeros de clase. Cuando ambos van caminando a la escuela, él habla mucho y suena sucio como una radio llena de cucarachas. Ustedes dos siempre toman el camino más largo porque el atajo los lleva bajo el puente George Washington, a través de un camino de cristales rotos y agujas, donde viven los zombis. Frankie dice que los zombis fuman *crack*. Los sabe todo esto porque tiene dos hermanos mayores. Uno está en la universidad, como tu padrastro, y el otro está en la cárcel por posesión de marihuana.

Frankie decide esperar para tomar el atajo después de la escuela. Después de la escuela, te encuentras con Frankie y lo sigues por el parque Fort Washington. Él ignora a los otros niños en las barras y los columpios. Notas dos columpios vacíos, pero Frankie no se detiene. Pregúntate si tienes miedo. ¿Lo tienes? La idea de tomar el atajo sin tu padrastro te da ganas de orinar. Pasas por el corral para perros y te preguntas qué está haciendo Queeny. Algunos perros ladran, otros husmean alrededor, y el resto corre en círculos.

Frankie se sienta en un banco que mira hacia New Jersey cuando llegas a la entrada trasera del parque. Comienza a hablar sobre dos aviones que se estrellaron contra el puente George Washington, y termina hablando de su hermano que lo llamó desde Rikers.

"¿Tiene miedo de ir a la cárcel?" preguntas.

"No. Sólo violan a los flacos".

"¿Tienes miedo de tomar el atajo?"

Frankie no responde. Patea un pañal por las escaleras.

Recuerdas que el teléfono de tu casa podría estar funcionando nuevamente, así que te pones de pie y sales del parque. Bajas corriendo las escaleras que conducen a la autopista. Con cada paso, los vidrios rotos crujen como copos de maíz. Casi resbalas en la basura congelada. Llegas a la acera junto a la autopista y ves una gran caja marrón debajo del andamio entre el puente George Washington y los edificios de Riverside Drive.

"Hay un zapato saliendo de la caja de allí", dice Frankie.

Coges una botella de plástico. Las tiras. La botella rebota y rueda por el pavimento agrietado. El zapato no se mueve.

"Mierda, Ray Ray, está muerto," dice Frankie.

Frankie y tú recogen todas las botellas y piedras que no están manchadas de mierda. Esperan: uno, dos...¡tres, Ataque! Las botellas se rompen y las piedras abollan la caja. Se detienen. La risa termina, y vuelven los zumbidos de los vehículos que pasan a toda velocidad por la autopista y el puente. La caja se queda quieta.

Caminas por la acera junto a la autopista. Hay un camino que se desvía hacia la calle que lleva a tu edificio en Riverside Drive. Los autos pasan rápido y cerca de este estrecho camino así que caminas debajo de los andamios donde viven los zombis. Los andamios son parte de una construcción abandonada al lado del puente. Hay pasamanos rotos, bancos quemados y tierra con el pavimento agrietado. Un zombi dobla una bolsa de basura, lo suficientemente grande para dos cuerpos, y te sonríe.

"Ese drogadicto no deja de mirarnos," dice Frankie. Se dan la vuelta antes de acercarse al zombi con la bolsa de basura gigante. Regresan a casa por el camino largo. Cuando llegan a las escaleras que conducen al parque Fort Washington, se dan cuenta de que no sale ningún zapato de la caja marrón.

"No está ahí porque está vivo," dice Frankie.

"Veamos qué hay dentro."

Coges una botella. Frankie está detrás de ti. Miras las escaleras que llevan al parque Fort Washington y al corral de perros y a tu escuela y a todo lo que es seguro. Tocas el cartón frío. Escuchas maullidos. Miras a través de un agujero mientras te tapas la nariz. No hay gatos. Das la vuelta y a unos metros de distancia hay un zombi, con un suéter negro roto, que tiene una piedra en la mano. Te congelas. Frankie sube corriendo las escaleras. El zombi lanza la piedra. Te agachas.

Frankie grita desde lo alto de las escaleras: "¡Tiene un cuchillo!"

Preocupación. Sujetas la sucia botella de vidrio con ambas manos. El zombi camina como si estuviera en una cuerda floja a punto de caerse. Cuanto más se acerca, más huele a orina y más ganas tienes de orinar. Escuchas que alguien te llama por tu nombre. Miras hacia las escaleras. Frankie se ha ido. Miras por encima de tu hombro. Sientes el viento frío de los vehículos que pasan. Imaginas que tu padrastro te está mirando y te espera para regañarte or tomar el atajo sin él. Tiras la botella. Rebota en el pecho del zombi. Subes corriendo las escaleras y tomas el camino más largo a casa.

Una brisa con hedor a mierda y orina sale del apartamento cuando empujas la puerta. Mary azota a Queeny con el cinturón de tu padrastro. Queeny corre hacia ti, gime con un rastro de sangre detrás de ella. Cada siete meses sangra. Los ojos de Mary están hinchados como si acabara de despertarse o terminara de llorar. No lleva maquillaje. La oscuridad bajo sus ojos parece sombra. Mientras Queeny tiembla entre tus piernas, te das cuenta de lo fea que se ha vuelto Mary.

"Este perro se va", grita Mary. "Nos vamos a deshacer de él hoy."

Náuseas. Te tapas la nariz. Todo esto se podría limpiar fácilmente: las gotas de sangre, los pedazos de zapatos, las esquinas mordidas del sofá, los escombros de mierda y los charcos de orina.

"Límpialo", dices.

Mary te arroja un zapato.

Te agachas y gritas: "Te odio".

Después de horas de llorar y de amenazas de escapar, te encuentras en Pinehurst Avenue, cerca de donde vive Olivia, una amiga de tu padrastro. Queeny camina atada con una correa delante de ti y de Mary.

"Aquí vive gente rica", dice Mary. "La adoptarán".

Sueltas la correa y esperas que Olivia la encuentre. Luego sigues a Mary sin miras atrás. Queeny te sigue, arrastrando su correa de metal sobre el concreto. erminas en Fort Washington Park y dejas a Queeny en el parquepara perros, allí se olvida de ti y persigue a los otros perros.

Esa noche, Mary te pregunta si quieres dormir con ella.

Le dices: 'Te odio', y te lames los labios, sintiendo el sabor salado de las lágrimas y los mocos.

"No podemos tener a esa perra. Estaba muerta de hambre," dice Mary, cerrando de un portazo la puerta del dormitorio.

~

Han pasado tres días y no te has suicidado. Tu padrastro no ha llamado. Frankie no ha ido a la escuela desde el día en que atacaste al zombi. La señora Vicioso dice que está enfermo. Has preguntado a los dueños de perros en Fort Washington Park sobre Queeny, pero nadie ha visto un perro de color marrón rojizo, de ojos color avellana. Parece un bulldog, pero en realidad es un mestizo.

Esta mañana, Mary te despertó para ir a la escuela acariciándote la cara porque sabe que estás molesto por lo de Queeny. Te acarició la cara en el hospital, aquella vez después de casi ahogarse en la bañera. La salvaste ese día sacando su cabeza del agua y sosteniéndola fuerte del cabello.

Después de la escuela encuentras a Nilda barriendo la cocina. Pasas por su lado y vas a la sala de estar. Te sientas en el sofá. Esperas a que ella diga algo. Ella dice algo. La ignoras. Ella arrastra la escoba hasta la sala, y se para debajo de la lámpara como un ángel-bruja con un resplandor sobre su cabeza.

"Lo siento por Queeny", dice.

"Queeny está muerta".

"Te equivocas, Ray. Adoptan perros como Queeny."

"No me patrocines."

"¿Qué?"

"No me patroncines."

"Quieres decir paternalices. ¿Crees que soy condescendiente contigo?"

"Depende".

Vas y te sientas a la mesa de la cocina, y miras por la ventana. Piensas en saltar. Nilda te lanza palabras mientras cocina espaguetis porque es el único alimento que queda.

"¡Derrame cerebral!" grita Nilda.

Tu dices: "Es como golpear, pero más fuerte, como un puñetazo"

Nilda niega con la cabeza y dice: "No, es un toque suave, como acariciar a un gato".

"¿No dijiste que fue un ataque al corazón?"

"No," dice dándote la espalda. "Es un toque suave. La siguiente palabra... Independiente".

"Ser soltero y feliz—"

Alguien toca a la puerta. Piensas en tu padrastro. Piensas en Queeny. Piensas en el amigo secreto de Nilda, Gregorio. Nilda revisa su celular. Ella gira la perilla de la estufa, y sale de la cocina. Piensas en saltar por la ventana, y romperte una pierna.

"Vamos, nena, ella no va a decir una mierda", dice el hombre en el pasillo.

"No puedo. Es mi trabajo", dice Nilda.

"Vamos, amor".

"Sólo por unos minutos".

La puerta se cierra. Las cerraduras hacen clic. Un hombre con una gorra de béisbol de los Yankees extiende su mano. Lo miras fijamente. Lleva una chaqueta de cuero, jeans y botas negras. Es más joven que tu padrastro.

"Hola, señor Rodríguez," dice el hombre.

"Éste es mi amigo, Nino," dice Nilda.

"Sí, su novio," dice el hombre.

Sientes algo raro en el pecho. Piensas en tu soplo cardíaco. Caries. Nilda dice que en cualquier lugar puedes tener caries, no solo en los dientes.

"¿Soñando despierto, señor Rodríguez?" pregunta el hombre con la mano extendida.

"Deja de llamarlo así". dice Nilda. "No está de humor".

Su amigo, Nino, dice que te ha visto por ahí. Dice que la mayoría de los perros callejeros son adoptados. Ignóralo. Sal de la cocina con tu plato.

Escuchas un fuerte susurro en la cocina.

"¿En serio estás pensando en ir?" pregunta Nino.

"Claro que sí", responde Nilda. "No tiene nada que ver con Greg".

"¿Qué pasa contigo y ese tal Greg?"

"Algunos de mis amigos son hombres".

"No he mencionado a Gregorio. ¿Por qué viajar tan lejos?"

"Porque quiero", dice Nilda en cuatro sílabas fuertes.

Los platos caen al fregadero con un golpe.

Despiertas en el sofá. El agua corre en la bañera. Nino se sienta en el otro extremo. Un libro de imágenes y una navaja descansan sobre su regazo.

"Señor Rodríguez", dice Nino arreglándose el cinturón. "¿Cree que guardar un secreto es importante si puede meter a alguien en problemas?"

Te frotas los ojos. No dices nada.

"¿Me meterías en problemas, señor Rodríguez?"

No lo entiendes. Te mantienes callado. Es un extraño.

"¿Alguna vez has pasado por debajo del puente?" pregunta Nino.

"No."

"¿Seguro que no has pasado por debajo de los andamios?"

"Sí... pero con mi padrastro. No puedo ir solo."

"Si delatas, señor Rodríguez..."

"¿Por qué me llamas así?"

"Respeto", dice Nino. Nilda dice que odias que te traten con condescendencia... "Iré al grano... No le dirás a Nilda que me viste debajo de los andamios porque no eres un chivato. Si Nilda se entera de que me viste, pensará que hice algo malo. Y si le digo a tu madre que te vi tirando botellas a los vagabundos, te meterás en problemas. Pero yo tampoco soy un soplón".

Asientes porque casi entiendes. Él cree que lo viste tomar el atajo debajo del puente.

"Usted guarda un secreto. Confío en usted, señor Rodríguez".

Nino hojea las páginas de *Where the Wild Things Are*. "Un chico solitario rodeado de monstruos suena como Beasts of No Nation."

Nino no parece alguien a quien le gusten los libros. Su sombrero está ahora echado hacia atrás. Es como esos tipos con ojos rojos que se apoyan con un pie en la pared y se

sientan en cajas de leche que están en la esquina, tipos como el hermano traficante de Frankie.

"Su mamá lo manda a la cama sin cenar", dice Nino.

"Ese libro es para niños pequeños", le dices. "¿Sabes lo de los soplos cardíacos?"

"¿Problema cardíaco?" dice Nino, rascándose los pocos pelos de su barbilla.

"Tengo uno. Mary dice que nací con un corazón extra pequeño".

"¿Quién es Mary?"

"Mi madre".

"Pareces saludable. Nilda dijo que querías huir de casa".

"A vece".

"Yo también". dice Nino, "pero quiero volver corriendo a casa de mis padres".

"¿Por qué?"

"Me echaron por vender... por... tomar el atajo".

"Hace mucho que no hablo con mi padrastro", dices.

"Leer te ayuda a no pensar en la gente que extrañas. Tienes que leer mucho para estar con una chica como Nilda".

No creas que Nino lee. Él no es como Nilda.

"Imagínate que tienes una novia con un nuevo amigo llamado Gregorio", dice Nino. "Ahora imagina que esa novia menciona que su nuevo amigo le prestó un libro aburrido llamado *School Days* de un tal Patrick-algo. Y tu novia dice que es mejor que el libro que te gusta, *Beasts of No Nation*."

"¿Ella piensa que el otro libro escolar es mejor que el libro de las bestias?" preguntas y tratas de no pensar en el amigo secreto de Nilda.

"Sí, eso es lo que piensa Nilda. Nunca terminó *Beasts of No Nation* porque es demasiado violento. Yo lo leí y me encantó, y ni siquiera me gusta leer. Nunca terminé *School Days* porque es aburrido. Me pregunto por qué le gusta tanto ese aburrido libro, *School Days*".

"¿Por qué no es violento?"

"No, no, está equivocado, señor Rodríguez. ¿Recuerdas que este amigo Gregorio le contó sobre el libro *School Days*?" Nino se comienza a limpiar sus uñas con la navaja. "¿Cómo te sentirías si finalmente lees un libro para impresionar a tu chica y ella ni siquiera lee el libro que leíste?"

"¿Estás celoso porque le gusta más el libro de Gregorio?"

"Mierda, eres listo... ¿Nilda te ha hablado de Gregorio?"

"No," dices, frotándote el pecho porque te duele el corazón cuando mientes, pero te dolería aún más si la delatas. "¿Nilda es tu novia o tu amiga?"

"Mi novia", murmura.

"¿Tienes miedo de que Gregorio sea más grande que tú?"

Nino se ríe. "Nunca tengo miedo. Puede que sea más alto, pero no más grande..."

Nilda sale del baño con el pelo alborotado. Ella pide mantas limpias. Nino se pone un dedo sobre los labios. Le dices que están sucias, y entras en el dormitorio. Nilda vuelve a tender la cama con la misma sábana sucia, incluso cuando

ya Mary había tendido la cama esa mañana. Cuando ella termina, te dejas caer en la cama. Debajo de una de las almohadas, hay una mancha húmeda que huele a cloro. Te duermes.

Te estás cayendo con Mary. Ella te sostiene la mano con fuerza. Hay un puente en el cielo. El viento se siente como una ducha fría. Sale vapor de la boca de Mary debido al frío que hace afuera o algo que está en lo profundo. La caída no es tan mala y se siente como un paseo en montaña rusa. Mientras caes en picada, notas dos objetos que caen debajo. Los dos objetos se acercan hasta que los pasas. Miras hacia arriba. Ves a tu padrastro y a Queeny flotando en el aire. Ambos cuerpos desaparecen. No puedes encontrar a Mary. Intentas volar. Sientes que estás nadando. Te ahogas. Tratas de salir a la superficie.

Te despiertas y hueles a Queeny. La lámpara se refleja en la pantalla del televisor, donde el único punto limpio es la huella de tu mano en una gruesa capa de polvo. El cesto de la ropa sucia está lleno y hay un charco de pantalones a su alrededor. Las cortinas cubren las dos ventanas de la salida de incendios. Estiras las piernas. No es a Queeny a lo que hueles, sino a tu propia orina. Mary se volverá loca cuando se entere.

Nilda podía secar la cama con un secador de pelo. Desde que visita sopresa de Nilda a Mary, ella se encarga de todo. Nilda vestía *jeans* negros y una camisa gris. Llevaba maquillaje, el pelo secado con secador y una identificación colgada de su cuello. Nilda escribió en un cuaderno negro y

preguntó sobre cómo llamaste al 911 y salvaste la vida de Mary cuando casi se ahoga en la bañera. Al principio, Mary te dijo que no le dijeras nada a Nilda porque iba a intentar llevarte. Pero Nilda ayudó a Mary a conseguir cupones de alimentos y un sofá cama, y cuida a los niños cada vez que Mary sale.

Si Nilda no seca la cama, Mary se volverá loca. Tus *jeans* se te pegan a las piernas. Casi te duchas, pero en vez de eso te cambias los *jeans*. La sala está oscura con la luz de la cocina. Nilda se fue. Mary ronca en el sofá como siempre. Probablemente olvidó que la reunión de padres y maestros es mañana. Te rascas los conductos lacrimales. La costra se te mete en las uñas. El piso cruje. Te muerdes las uñas. Corres porque se volvió loca la última vez que mojaste la cama. Te pones el abrigo. Miras a Mary soñando antes de irte. La agarras de la muñeca y tocas tu cara con su mano. Su reloj marca las 11:30p.m. Hay un agujero entre sus fosas nasales. Tose y jadea en busca de aire. Aprieta su corazón como el hombre de la ambulancia. Tose. No abre los ojos, como cuando la sacaste de la bañera.

Mary dice: "¿Chris?" pero no se despierta.

Es de noche, pero Riverside Drive no da miedo. No es como la mañana, cuando no hay coches estacionados. El amarillo en las ventanas del apartamento te dice quién está despierto. A veces puedes ver las sombras de las familias en las paredes y los techos. Cruzas las calles desiertas en el frío oscuro. Los vientos están furiosos en Pinehurst Avenue. Dejas

de toser. No puedes. Sigues tosiendo. Los mocos te resbalan por la nariz congestionada. Ojalá tuvieras un agujero entre las fosas nasales como Mary.

¡Sorpresa! Ralph está frente al edificio de Olivia. El tipo gordo de New Jersey, que solía llevar comida a tu casa, pero desapareció cuando tu padrastro se fue a la universidad, está sentado en la entrada con bolsas de compras. Se está quedando dormido como un zombi. Pero Ralph es demasiado gordo para ser un zombi. Si Ralph te ve, te delatará y se lo dirá a tu padrastro. Vuelves corriendo a casa.

Subes corriendo las escaleras de tu edificio. Esperando que tu padrastro no haya llamado.

Mary bloquea la puerta del apartamento. "¿Dónde has estado?"

"En ninguna parte."

"¿Quieres que le diga a Chris que te escapaste porque mojaste la cama?"

Las cutículas de tu dedo medio te molestan. Si te las arrancas con los dientes, arden. "Vi a Ralph llevando comida al edificio de Olivia."

"¿Qué?" pregunta Mary. "¿Ralph el grande?"

"Sí."

"Vamos," dice ella.

Cuando Mary y tú llegan a Pinehurst Avenue, ella te dice que te quedes al otro lado de la calle del edificio de Olivia. Te deja su teléfono celular y te dice que llames a la policía si pasa algo. Mary entra al edificio de Olivia. Ojalá, Ralph, llevara

comida a tu casa. Piensas en cómo los postes de luz brillan del color de la orina. Miras la luna. No parece que esté hecha de queso.

Mary sale corriendo del edificio de Olivia con dos bolsas de la compra. "Vamos," dice. "Déjame coger el teléfono."

Sigues el ritmo de Mary mientras habla por el celular.

"¿Contestador automático, Ralph? Gordo pedazo de mierda. Si te encuentro en Heights comprándole a esa asesina, Olivia, haré que Chris te corte las pelotas cuando salga. Podría haberte conseguido lo que necesitabas como solía hacer Chris, pero vas a donde Olivia a mis espaldas..."

"¿Por qué estás molesta con Ralph?"

"Es un drogadicto," dice ella. "No quiero que estés cerca de drogadictos."

A la mañana siguiente te despiertas solo en el dormitorio. Mary no te despertó para ir a la escuela, pero nunca lo hace. Escuchas a un hombre en la sala de estar. Piensas en tu padrastro.

Nino está en el sofá, hablando por su celular. "...No te lo voy a echar en cara. Le estoy haciendo un favor al chico, no a ti... Estudiar en el extranjero no es estudiar. La gente viaja para follar". Nino te ve, se pone un dedo sobre los labios y cuelga.

"¿Mary está en el hospital?"

"No, tu mamá está haciendo diligencias y Nilda está en el trabajo".

"Estoy tarde para la escuela."

"No te perderás nada, hoy es medio día. No le digas a Nilda que te dejé quedarte en casa... ¿Tienes hambre? Pedí comida china para desayunar".

"Es medio día porque hoy es la reunión de padres y maestros".

"Lo sé," dice. "Nilda y tu mamá no volverán hasta más tarde, así que te llevaré".

Al anochecer, Nino y tú toman el atajo hacia la escuela. Uno de los zombis grita desde debajo de los andamios: "¡Arturo!"

Nino levanta una mano y dice: "Seco".

Cuando llegas al pie de las escaleras que llevan al parque Fort Washington, le preguntas a Nino: "¿Por qué Nilda ayuda a mi familia?"

"Es su trabajo. Además, le recuerdas a su primo Juan."

"¿Juan tiene un perro?"

"No".

"¿Juan fue lateral izquierdo?"

"No lo sé. Tal vez. La universidad comunitaria es como ser lateral izquierdo".

"¿Juan nació con un soplo cardíaco?"

"No estoy seguro, señor Rodríguez".

"¿La madre de Juan intentó suicidarse?"

"La madre de Juan murió por tomar drogas" dice Nino, limpiándose las uñas con la navaja.

La luna está afuera cuando llegas al parque vacío de Fort Washington. No hay niños fugitivos en el patio de juegos ni

perros fugitivos sin ndueño. Los columpios cuelgan inmóviles, como si estuvieran congelados en el tiempo. Puedes ver a través de las barras de mono. No hay fila para el tobogán grande. Nino y tú se sientan en un banco junto a la fuente de agua porque llegaste temprano. No hay estrellas, solo la luz roja de un avión en el cielo.

"Nilda dijo que se va a España".

"Lo sé". Nino abre mucho los ojos, como si necesitaran aire.

"¿Vendes drogas?"

"Conozco gente que está en la cárcel por vender drogas" dice Nino.

"Ese vagabundo te llamó Arturo. ¿Tienes diferentes nombres para distintas personas?"

"Sí, y diferentes secretos" dice Nino. "Señor Rodríguez, si supieras que Nilda tiene otro novio, ¿me lo dirías?"

"Depende".

Cuando entras a la escuela, Nino sale para hablar con la señora Vicioso y te deja en el gimnasio, donde no hay adultos. Hay niños grandes que lanzan pelotas de baloncesto a niños más pequeños, y niños y niñas debajo de las gradas. Una niña con un abrigo rosa estrangula a una niña con un abrigo azul. Un niño corre hacia ti, grita y luego sale corriendo, deja un zapato atrás. Dos niños aúllan a las luces del techo.

Te sientas en las gradas, ignorando los sonidos de besos debajo de ti y observas a los padres dejar a sus hijos en la escuela. Frankie entra al gimnasio con su padre. Su padre

parece viejo y estúpido porque no sabe inglés. Frankie es un mentiroso que te abandonó. Tu padrastro mataría al padre de Frankie en una pelea. Al padre de Frankie no le importa Frankie porque lo deja con todos estos niños locos en el gimnasio. Frankie corre por el gimnasio y cuanto más se acerca, más se parece a su padre.

"Hablé con mi hermano," dice Frankie. "No está en Rikers. Está en el programa S.H.O.C.K., como una prisión militar. Vio a tu padre. Hay un sargento instructor con un tatuaje en el brazo de un bebé negro colgado de una cuerda que les obliga a hacer flexiones..."

"No es mi padre. Es mi padrastro y está en la universidad".

"No es una universidad de verdad, como la de mi otro hermano. Solo les permiten hacer un examen para obtener el diploma".

"Deja de mentir".

Le das un puñetazo a Frankie en la cara. Él camina hacia atrás, llorando como un pendejo. Frankie se cubre la nariz con la sangre que gotea entre sus dedos. Podría desangrarse hasta morir. Se forma una multitud alrededor de ustedes dos. Corres hacia la salida de la puerta trasera. ¡Date prisa!

Cruzas corriendo la calle hasta el parque vacío de Fort Washington. La policía te arrestará. Piensas en ahogarte en el río Hudson. Bajas corriendo las escaleras hasta la autopista. Haces una pausa al pie de las escaleras. Al otro lado de los ocho carriles de la autopista hay otro parque y, después de él, el río Hudson. Piensas antes de cruzar. Sientes el viento de los

coches que pasan a toda velocidad, como si estuvieran corriendo en una carrera.

Alguien te agarra el brazo. Gritas.

"Dame dinero".

"No tengo nada".

El zombi te hace una llave en el cuelloa y presiona un metal frío en tu garganta. Revisa tus bolsillos. "Te arrancaré el corazón".

"Nací con un soplo en el corazón".

Cierras los ojos. Rezas a tu padrastro. El zombi se aleja volando. Nino lo arroja al suelo. Salta sobre él, lo estrangula con una mano y sostiene su navaja con la otra.

"No apuñales al zombi, Nino".

Nino te mira. Mira al zombi antes de soltarlo.

De camino a casa suena el celular de Nino.

"Sí, estaba en el parque" dice. "Su madre te llamará."

Nino no te pregunta por qué golpeaste a Frankie.

"Hagamos un trato, señor Rodríguez. Si no dejas que Nilda se vaya a España, prometo no contarle a nadie lo de esta noche. ¿Trato?"

"Está bien, pero dime… ¿Mi padrastro está en la cárcel por vender drogas?"

"Sí, Raymond," dice Nino y te acaricia la cabeza. "Lo siento."

Créele a Nino. Tu padrastro está en la cárcel. No quieres delatar a Nilda, pero prefieres ser un soplón que ocultarle algo a Nino. Así que le cuentas lo de Gregorio.

"Señor Rodríguez, no tiene que fingir que conoce al amigo de Nilda. De todos modos, no le contaré a nadie lo de esta noche".

No le cuentas nada más a Nino sobre Gregorio porque hieres sus sentimientos. No te cree porque no quiere creer.

A la mañana siguiente, los ronquidos de Mary te despiertan en tu dormitorio. Es sábado, pero no tienes ganas de ver dibujos animados. En una ventana, la cortina está a medio bajar para que veas el polvo que trae el sol. En la otra ventana, la cortina está completamente bajada para que no haya polvo. Es mejor tener las cortinas bajadas porque el polvo hace estornudar.

El celular de Mary vibra en el suelo.

"¿Hola?"

"¿Aceptas la llamada a cobro revertido de Christian Ruiz?" pregunta una voz robótica.

"Sí."

"Hola," dice una voz ronca.

Parece que tu padrastro está llorando. Quédate callado. Escucha.

"Siento no haber llamado," dice. "No quería..."

"Nilda dice que los hombres lloran... ¿Sabes que Queeny se ha ido?"

"Escuché. ¿Es Nilda la mujer de Servicios Infantiles?"

"Sí. Ayudó a Mary a conseguir un trabajo, pero Mary enfermó y lo perdió".

Tu padrastro tose. "Si Mary está durmiendo dale un beso".

Frotas tu nariz contra la de Mary y huele a cigarrillos. Te encanta el olor. Recuerdas cómo se reía con un cigarrillo en la boca, con un ojo entrecerrado por el humo. Tocas sus labios. La sequedad se siente como plástico roto. Lames los labios de tu madre.

"¿Estás dibujando?" pregunta.

"Sí, estoy calcando los tuyos".

"No puedes calcar mis dibujos ni tomar el atajo".

"¿Estás en la cárcel por vender drogas?"

Se aclara la garganta. "Hijo, te dije que estoy en la escuela".

Y aunque Frankie, Nino y la voz dentro de ti dicen que tu padrastro está en la cárcel, decides creerle. Él está en la universidad.

EN LAS PANTALLAS

"Las personas publican citas de Baldwin, pero no lo leen."
— *Marwa Helal*

El 23 de marzo de 2024 falleció mi padrastro. Escribo esto cuatro meses después. Las elecciones presidenciales de Estados Unidos han copado el ciclo informativo. Dicen que la democracia depende de un hilo. Rusia ataca a Ucrania, Estados Unidos financia a Ucrania. Israel comete un genocidio en Palestina, Estados Unidos financia a Israel. Veo los rostros de niños palestinos que están siendo desenterrados de los escombros de los edificios bombardeados. Tantos niños muertos, como en una película de terror: una pantalla entre el genocidio y yo.

El 17 de mayo de 2023, un año antes de su muerte, mi padrastro me envió un mensaje de texto: <<Hola, por favor, responde. Es importante. Estoy en problemas; necesito ayuda>>. Ese mismo día, Donald Trump, el favorito para la nominación republicana del 2024 en ese momento, se atribuyó el mérito de que la Corte Suprema de Estados Unidos revocara a Roe v. Wade. En las redes sociales, publicó:

<<Pude anular a Roe v. Wade>>. Ese mismo día, el congresista Bill Foster, demócrata de Illinois, volvió a presentar la Ley de Ampliación de Oportunidades para la Recuperación que permitiría a los estados recibir subvenciones a través del Centro para el Tratamiento del Abuso de Sustancias. El dinero ampliaría los esfuerzos de prevención del uso de sustancias y tratamientos que funcionan, basados en evidencia, incluido el tratamiento asistido con medicamentos. El titular del comunicado de prensa del congresista Foster decía: <<Foster presenta una legislación para combatir la epidemia de opioides>>. Más tarde ese día, mi hermana me envió un mensaje de texto diciéndome que mi padrastro —su padre— necesitaba el dinero para heroína. Le respondí: <<Lo sé>>.

En dos meses cumpliré cuarenta. Pensé que sería capaz de entender las interminables alertas de noticias de último momento en mi teléfono y observar sin absorber. Pero es todo lo contrario. Cuanto más me acerco a los cuarenta, más confusas son las noticias, sin importar si son de la ciudad de Nueva York, los Apalaches, Bangladesh, Palestina, la República Democrática del Congo o Sudán. Por la noche, la necesidad de coherencia me mantiene despierto en la cama. Mi mente intenta crear una sola historia a partir de horas de navegación en *Instagram, TikTok* y *YouTube*. Detrás de mis párpados hay un juego de azar. Una máquina tragamonedas con tres carretes que giran. Los carretes muestran una variedad errática de todas las imágenes que he visto, ya sea

con mis propios ojos o en una pantalla. No hay un premio gordo que ganar porque el giro nunca se detiene. Ninguna combinación de imágenes en mi cabeza conduce a un significado. Simplemente me despierto cansado al día siguiente.

Darle sentido al ciclo de noticias diarias no es diferente a darle sentido a tu vida cuando te das cuenta de que tienes más años a tus espaldas que por delante. Puedes organizar las imágenes en tu cabeza cronológicamente para crear un significado, pero eso no garantiza que entenderás nada de lo que viste o viviste. Cuanto más viejo me hago, más fragmentadas se vuelven mis notas autobiográficas. No puedo decirte si lo que recuerdo es una memoria de la infancia, una escena de una película o un libro, o algo que vi en alguna pantalla. En un discurso titulado *The Artist's Struggle for Identity*, James Baldwin habla sobre la vida del poeta y el artista. Dice: <<Y de alguna manera terrible, que supongo que nadie puede describir jamás, te ves obligado, acorralado, azotado para que te enfrentes a lo que sea que te haya lastimado>>. En este momento, no puedo distinguir la vida que he vivido desde la proyección retrospectiva de los acontecimientos en mi mente, un *en-memoria* de todas las personas que he conocido y todas las personas que he sido. ¿Cuántas veces he revisado el principio y el final de mi propia historia?

Salto atrás en el tiempo a recuerdos donde, en una noche helada, camino por Fort Washington Avenue hacia el puente

George Washington, listo para volar. No pude terminar la novela *Another Country* en mis dos primeros intentos. Hoy, pienso en uno de los personajes, Rufus Scott, y en cómo él tuvo éxito donde yo fracasé. Scott es un baterista de jazz afroamericano que se suicida, saltando del puente George Washington. No puedo distinguir mis pensamientos de esa noche y el suicidio de Scott en la novela de Baldwin. Recuerdo que estaba en la ruina. Entonces, llamé a mi padrastro, quien me envió dinero al día siguiente. Nunca tuvimos una conversación honesta sobre mi ideación suicida y su trastorno por consumo de sustancias. Incluso cuando me felicitó por un logro como escritor, nunca hablamos del pasado en el que se basaba mi ficción; una historia que compartimos.

~

En *The Devil Finds Work*, Baldwin reseña la película *The Exorcist* (1973). No está convencido de que una niña poseída de doce años, interpretada por Regan, que se masturba con un crucifijo, sea una representación realista del mal. Afirma que la película prioriza los efectos especiales sobre la condenación real y explica: <<Porque he visto al diablo, de día y de noche, y lo he visto en ti y en mí: en los ojos del policía, el alguacil y el sustituto del alguacil, el arrendador, la ama de casa, el jugador de fútbol; en los ojos de algunos drogadictos, en los ojos de algunos predicadores, en los ojos de algunos

gobernadores, presidentes, guardianes, en los ojos de algunos huérfanos, y en los ojos de mi padre, y en mi espejo>>. Para Baldwin, la representación del mal que hace la película ignora el mal real, el mal no reconocido de la sociedad estadounidense.

De niño, veía películas de terror con mis padres, pero no recuerdo haber visto *The Exorcist*. Conozco la imagen de la niña poseída que se eleva desde la cama, maldiciendo a los sacerdotes y jugando con el crucifijo. Al ver la película de adulto, me reí cuando la niña poseída de doce años le dijo al sacerdote Damien Karras: <<Tu madre chupa bolas en el infierno, Karras, baboso desleal>>. Karras está atormentado por la culpa porque no estuvo presente cuando su madre falleció sola en un pequeño apartamento. En otro momento, el demonio le dice: << ¡Mataste a tu madre! ¡La dejaste morir sola! ¡Bastardo!>> Baldwin escribe: <<Esta culpa inquietante e incluso aterrorizada es el subtexto de *The Exorcist*, que, sin embargo, no puede exorcizarla porque nunca la enfrenta>>.

Ojalá hubiera visto *The Exorcist* con mis padres. Mi madre de veinticuatro años y mi padrastro de diecinueve me dejaban ver cualquier película, siempre y cuando me quejara y suplicara. Si no vi ninguna película para mayores de diecisiete años con ellos, no fue porque me protegieran de las blasfemias o los efectos especiales, sino porque tenía miedo y no quería verla.

Me hubiese gustado que me hubieran expuesto a los horrores de sus vidas, así como me dejaron ver películas

clasificadas R. A los ocho años, veía lo que estaba pasando a nuestro lado de la pantalla. No importaba lo que oía de los adultos de mi familia y de la escuela, solo creía lo que veía. Las sustancias que alteraban el estado de ánimo o drogas estaban por todo mi vecindario, estaban en mi familia: aspirina, café, nicotina, etc. Cerveza y licor. Y, sin embargo, en el apartamento en el que vivía y en la escuela a la que asistía, solo me decían: <<Simplemente di que no>>. Si alguien me ofrecía drogas, tenía que decir que no. Basándome en los anuncios de servicio público que veía sobre las drogas, tenía la impresión de que alguien en la calle me iba a llevar a un callejón y me obligaría a consumir drogas contra mi voluntad. Eso nunca sucedió. Todas las drogas que he consumido, las he consumido con entusiasmo. La última vez que luché contra el consumo de drogas, probablemente, era un bebé tomando medicinas con una cuchara.

No había transparencia. No había ninguna conversación. Lo único que sabía sobre las drogas eran los <<efectos secundarios>>. Veía a alcohólicos, drogadictos, adictos al crac, piperos, tecatos. Y los llamaba así. Los adultos llamaban a estas personas así. Juzgaba a las personas que no eran lo suficientemente fuertes para decir que <<no>> y eran demasiado débiles para dejar de fumar de golpe y salvarse. De niño, nunca reconocí a quienes "funcionaban" y consumían fuera de la vista, en secreto o durante los fines de semana. En mi mente, cuando una persona fallaba en decirle que <<no>> a las drogas, se transformaba instantáneamente en alguien

con un trastorno por consumo de sustancias. Los consumidores ocasionales, los influenciados por su entorno social, los experimentadores no existían. Las drogas eran malignas. Hasta el día de hoy, así es como muchos adultos les hablan a los adolescentes sobre las drogas. Las instrucciones son: dile que no a las drogas. Y la solución para quienes tienen un trastorno por consumo de sustancias es: solo deja de consumir.

En mi adolescencia, supe que mis padres consumían drogas, pero nunca hablé con ellos al respecto. Ellos nunca me hablaron de ello. Durante muchos años, esto no me afectó porque no se podía ver en sus ojos. Era un secreto. Pero lo supe mucho antes de que fuera obvio. Personalmente sabía lo que Baldwin quería decir cuando escribió: <<Los niños, que aún no son conscientes de que es peligroso mirar demasiado profundo a cualquier cosa, miran todo, se miran entre sí y sacan sus propias conclusiones>>.

Como adulto, lamento no haberles hablado de la realidad que hay de nuestro lado de la pantalla. Nunca los cuestioné. Soy consciente de que, incluso si los hubiera enfrentado como adulto, no tenía garantizada la verdad ni su supervivencia. Pero como dijo Baldwin, <<No todo lo que se enfrenta se puede cambiar, pero nada se puede cambiar a menos que se enfrente>>.

Alquilabamos cintas VHS en el Blockbuster de la calle 178 y Broadway. También las alquilamos en una pequeña tienda de VHS en la calle 186 y St. Nicholas, donde hoy se encuentra

el *All Star Barbershop*. No recuerdo dónde alquilamos *Faces of Death* (1978). La vimos en el dormitorio de mis padres. No recuerdo que mis padres me dijeran que era demasiado joven para ver una película. Una vez metí el dedo en un frasco de azúcar y me froté el azúcar en las encías. Estaba imitando a Christopher Walken o Lawerence Fishburn en *King of New York* (1990). Mi madre llamó a mi padrastro y me pidió que lo hiciera de nuevo. Me negué, por supuesto. Nunca me dijeron que no lo hiciera, pero sabía que no debía volver a hacerlo. La noche en que vimos *Faces of Death*, no conocía la muerte. Mi bisabuela estaba viva para ese entonces. Mi madre estaba viva. Mi padrastro estaba vivo. Cuando volví a ver la película recientemente, me enteré de que no era un documental. Durante años, recomendé *Faces of Death* a la gente como un documental sobre cadáveres y personas que comen cerebros de mono. Digo cadáveres, pero me refiero a los rostros. La muerte está en el rostro. No importa si alguien sufre una sobredosis, se suicida, muere de cáncer o de vejez. En cuanto el corazón se detiene, el rostro cambia inmediatamente. Un funerario de mano dura. Un funerario amable. No hace ninguna diferencia. No hay máscara para la muerte. Muchas vidas después de haber visto la película por primera vez, aprendí que *Faces of Death* no es un documental, sino una película de horror mondo. Mondo es un subgénero del cine documental explotador, pseudo documentales sensacionalistas hechos con material archivado y escenas montadas. Retratan culturas fuera de los Estados Unidos,

centrándose en temas como la muerte y el sexo.

Durante años, imaginé que había recibido algún tipo de educación. Juraba que *Faces of Death* me había enseñado algo sobre la muerte, cosas que otros niños de diez años no sabían. ¿Qué exactamente imaginé? No lo sé. Recién acabo de enterarme, a dos meses de cumplir cuarenta años, de que esta película que he estado recomendando no es un documental. Aprendí esto mucho después de la muerte de mi bisabuela en la República Dominicana. Ocho años después de que mi madre falleciera en Cali, Colombia. Unos meses después de la muerte de mi padrastro en Jersey City.

Durante mucho tiempo, pensé que sabía algo sobre el mundo que otros niños no sabían porque yo sí veía películas clasificadas R con mis padres. Nunca consideré que el hecho de que mi madre casi sufriera una sobredosis cuando estaba en séptimo grado fuera una lección. Visitar a mi padrastro en la cárcel nunca me reveló nada. Sin embargo, estaba seguro de que *Faces of Death*, una película de terror me enseñó sobre la muerte.

De niño, veía todos los géneros con mis padres, pero sobre todo recuerdo todas las películas de terror que veíamos. En *Anatomy of Genres*, John Truby dice que el género de terror gira en torno a los <<pecados del pasado>>. Pienso en cómo no respondí al último mensaje de texto que mi madre me envió. Dios ordenó que los hijos obedezcan y honren a sus padres, y que no hay pecado más grande que ignorar el mensaje de texto de tu madre, especialmente si está en otro

país pidiéndote que le envíes dinero. Eso me suena como a la premisa de una película de terror. El protagonista no responde al mensaje de texto de su madre y desde entonces ha estado atormentado por eso. Entonces escribe sobre películas de terror, en vez del mensaje de texto que no envió.

Recuerdo *Dr. Giggles* (1992). Un psicópata que se cree médico regresa al pueblo donde mataron a su padre y comienza a matar gente. Recuerdo *Candyman* (1992). El fantasma vengativo de un hombre brutalmente asesinado por amar a una mujer blanca a fines del siglo XIX aparece cuando dices su nombre cinco veces en el espejo. Veíamos estas películas de terror en VHS. Me sentaba en el piso, de espaldas hacia la cama. Me ponía frente al televisor, la única luz en el dormitorio. Mi madre y mi padrastro miraban desde la cama. Siempre me sorprendía la brusquedad de un ruido fuerte y el cambio de visuales en la pantalla durante los sustos repentinos. Estaba atemorizado. Miraba a mis padres. Me preocupaba que notaran el miedo en mis ojos y reconocieran la vergüenza que sentía. Pero mis padres no me prestaban atención. Ni siquiera estaban allí. Estaban perdidos en la película. Dos rostros jóvenes y hermosos brillaban en el televisor, inmersos en el terror.

~

La meta era que los estudiantes escribieran sobre sí mismos. No preguntaron, pero les dije que la palabra <<ensayo>> viene del francés <<intentar o probar>>. Agregué que también en español <<ensayo>> significa una práctica de una obra de teatro, película u otra producción posterior a la grabación y/o presentación en público. Mencioné el ensayo de Walter Benjamin, en el que escribe sobre estar drogado con hachís en algún lugar de Francia. Escuchamos y leímos *One Love* de Nas. Había olvidado que estos estudiantes no eran adolescentes a principios del siglo XX. No eran yo, un adolescente a principios de los 2000s.

La tarea consistía en escribir lo que recordaban del día anterior. Cuando me decían que no sabían qué escribir, citaba a Baldwin: <<Cuando escribes, intentas averiguar algo que no sabes...>>

Cuando enseñaba, no había pizarrones inteligentes en todos los salones de clase de secundaria. Si había un pizarrón inteligente con *YouTube* que reproducía fragmentos de entrevistas de Baldwin. Algunas escuelas bloquearon *YouTube*. El mismo *YouTube* que tienen en sus teléfonos móviles y en casa.

Los videos de Baldwin paseando por las calles llamaron su atención. Les enseñé un clip donde Baldwin le dice a Dick Cavett: <<Tal vez no creo que esta República sea la cumbre de la civilización humana. Tal vez no quiero convertirme en Ronald Reagan o en el presidente de *General Motors*. Tal vez tengo otro sentido de la vida en el que, de hecho, mi situación

aquí me ha obligado a confiar. Y tal vez sé más sobre ti y tus instituciones de lo que tú sabes sobre mí. Y tal vez tengo un juicio sobre ellas. Tal vez no quiero lo que crees que quiero. Tal vez hay algo que puedo darte...>>

Para la mayoría de los adolescentes a los que atendí, no había manera de pasar del video a la lectura. Querían seguir viendo a Baldwin en *YouTube*. Y yo también quería seguir viéndolo. Quería dique <<atestiguar>>, haciendo un seguimiento del algoritmo. Imágenes consecutivas de todo en todas partes. Podría pasar horas viendo clips de Baldwin, fingiendo que estaba investigando.

Cuando mis alumnos se quejaban de que preferían seguir viendo videos de Baldwin en lugar de leer, yo me quejaba de que las redes sociales están destruyendo su capacidad de atención. Admito que hoy día apenas puedo leer. Cuanto más mayor me hago, más difícil me resulta leer a Baldwin o a cualquier otro escritor. Es más fácil cuando leo en voz alta o leo mientras escucho el audiolibro al mismo tiempo. Leer siempre me ha resultado difícil, pero ahora me parece imposible. Las palabras que antes evocaban su significado literal ahora desencadenan un lío de connotaciones.

~

Actualmente, estoy trabajando mi último verano en un programa extraescolar en Harlem. Después de dejar el Departamento de Educación, comencé a trabajar para una organización sin fines de lucro que brinda apoyo integral las veinticuatro horas del día, los siete días de la semana, a jóvenes afroamericanos y latinos. Es mi última vez en este programa porque, después de cuatro años con la organización, he comenzado a tener recuerdos del pasado. De repente, no estoy hablando con una chica afroamericana de dieciséis años del Bronx, sino con mi madre adolescente. Estar completamente presente entre los adolescentes a los que atiendo me transporta al pasado almacenado dentro de mí. Entonces, tengo que fingir que no es mi madre quien me habla sobre por qué se escabulló del taller para ir al baño a hacer un video de baile de *TikTok*. Tengo que fingir que no es mi padrastro y que es un chico dominicano de quince años recién llegado de Capotillo, Santo Domingo.

En un invierno cálido, mi co-facilitador y yo estábamos en *Riverbank Park* con nuestro grupo de adolescentes. Poco a poco se fueron uniendo a nosotros jóvenes provenientes de escuelas secundarias de toda la ciudad de New York. Una chica adolescente estaba sentada en un banco frente a mi co-facilitador y a mí. Ella jugaba con papas fritas y una hamburguesa con queso. Dijo que las papas fritas sabían a helado. Estábamos hablando de alternativas a las cárceles cuando nos recordó que su padre estuvo en prisión durante diez años. Lo sabíamos, pero no sabíamos por qué. Sin previo

aviso, mientras hablábamos de Kalief Browder y comíamos papas fritas blandas, nos dijo que su padre le disparó al hombre que abusó de ella.

Este es el mal del que Baldwin dijo que *The Exorcist* no logró explorar. Mi co-facilitador y yo continuamos escuchando a la adolescente. Ella habló con total naturalidad sobre su historia. En un momento dado, la chica se aburrió de nosotros y se levantó para mostrarle su teléfono celular a otro adolescente. Mi co-facilitador y yo nos miramos, anticipando nuestro informe de fin de día.

Mientras la adolescente hablaba sobre su padre, se convirtió en mi madre. Ella tenía la misma edad que mi madre cuando me dio a luz. No tengo idea de lo que pasó mi madre cuando era niña.

La autopsia y el informe toxicológico del actor Heath Ledger concluyeron que murió <<como resultado de una intoxicación aguda por los efectos combinados de oxicodona, hidrocodona, diazepam, temazepam, alprazolam y doxilamina>>. No soy un experto, pero no puedo evitar pensar que fueron las benzodiazepinas las que lo mataron. Deprimen el sistema nervioso, reduciendo la respiración y acercándote al sueño eterno.

Cuando pienso en Heath Ledger, no pienso en su rol como el *Joker* y en su trágica muerte, como lo hacen la mayoría de las personas. Pienso en cómo el actor fue encontrado con un guion de película. Según el director Stephen Gaghan, Ledger iba a protagonizar la adaptación de Malcolm Gladwell,

Blink: The Power of Thinking Without Thinking. El libro trata sobre las primeras impresiones y la ciencia de juzgar rápidamente. Supuestamente, el director Stephen Gaghan estaba obsesionado con el capítulo sobre las emociones que profundiza en cómo algunas personas son buenas para saber de inmediato lo que sienten o piensan los demás. Tenía esta habilidad con mi madre cuando era niño, pero a medida que me hice mayor, las cosas cambiaron. Y no sé si es que perdí mi don o si con el paso de los tiempos ella misma perdió la capacidad de saber lo que sentía o pensaba.

Después de la muerte de mi madre, mientras buscaba en su apartamento en Cali, Colombia, encontré en su bolso la versión en español del libro de Osho, *Fear: Understanding and Accepting the Insecurities of Life*. Todavía no lo he abierto. También tengo una copia de *Tuesdays with Morrie* de Mitch Albom. Mi madre dijo que el libro le recordaba mi relación con mi bisabuela. Todavía no lo he leído. A veces, me imagino muriéndome sin haber leído estos libros. Otro texto que siguió a mi madre fue *The Pill Book: The Illustrated Guide to the Most Prescribed Drugs in the United States*. Mi madre tenía una copia cuando vivíamos en Riverside Drive, cerca de la calle 181. Era una edición antigua, hecha jirones y desgastada. Cuando vi el libro de niño, me recordó a la Biblia. La edición de bolsillo de la 15 edición tiene 1,296 páginas.

En la canción *Sometimes I Rhyme Slow* de Nice & Smooth, Smooth rapea sobre una amante del pasado. Mientras el rapero estaba de gira, la amante chocó su auto. Él

descubre que ella estaba husmeando en su Mercedes Benz. Él rapea: <<Pasó el tiempo y comencé a notar la pérdida de peso/Entonces tuve que preguntarle si estaba montando el caballo blanco>>. Durante mucho tiempo pensé que la etimología de la jerga <<caballo blanco>> tenía que ver con el Libro de las Revelaciones.

En el último libro de la Biblia, la Muerte cabalga sobre un caballo pálido como el cuarto y último jinete del Apocalipsis. Según la versión de King James:

<<Y miré, y he aquí un caballo pálido; y el que lo montaba tenía por nombre Muerte; y el Infierno lo seguía. Y se les dio potestad sobre la cuarta parte de la tierra, para matar con espada, con hambre, con mortandad y con las fieras de la tierra>>.

En 2024, cuando tomo el metro de la MTA, me siento como si estuviera en el Libro de las Revelaciones. Veo cuerpos en el andén, y no puedo decir si están vivos o muertos. No es que me importe porque estoy más preocupado por mis otros compañeros de viaje. Hay titulares sobre personas que son empujadas en las vías del tren, así que estoy listo para defender mi vida.

Estoy escribiendo esto durante un año de elecciones presidenciales y, según las redes sociales y los medios de comunicación tradicionales, mi voto determinará si avanzamos o no hacia el final. En las redes sociales, sigo a amigos que atacan a personas que no publican sobre el genocidio de Israel contra el pueblo palestino. Silencio en la

violencia. Mientras tanto, ambas partes en conflicto en Sudán (las Fuerzas de Apoyo Rápido y las Fuerzas Armadas Sudanesas) han sido acusadas de violación y violación en grupo. El año pasado, el conflicto en el este de la República Democrática del Congo cumplió treinta años. Los resultados electorales han declarado a Nicolás Maduro presidente de Venezuela. En las redes sociales, o eres un intervencionista que apoya a la derecha y al imperio estadounidense o un comunista que apoya a la dictadura. En medio de todo esto, Joe Biden abandonó su carrera presidencial, convirtiendo a Kamala Harris en la candidata presidencial demócrata. Demócratas y Republicanos por igual apoyan y financian el genocidio. Las imágenes de bebés y niños muertos ya no son motivo de sustos repentinos. ¿Mencioné que Trump sobrevivió a un intento de asesinato?

Estamos en agosto de 2024, y la última cohorte de estudiantes a los que enseñé en el Departamento de Educación tiene poco más de veinte años. Todos los jóvenes a los que enseñé tienen edad para votar. Me pregunto si están perdiendo el sueño con las elecciones estadounidenses o el genocidio que comete Israel contra el pueblo de Gaza. Me imagino a uno de ellos diciéndome algo sobre <<el menor de los dos males>>. Me pregunto cuántos han llegado a un punto que Baldwin describe en *The Struggle of the Artist*, donde dice: <<...la mayoría de nosotros, blancos y negros, hemos llegado a un punto en el que todavía creemos, insistimos y actuamos según los principios, lo cual ya no es válido, que esto

es tan óptimo, que nuestra elección es el menor de dos males, y esto ya no es cierto. La gonorrea no es preferible a la sífilis>>.

Me alegro de que ya no sean adolescentes, y de que yo ya no sea su profesor porque no quiero contaminarlos. Recuerdo haber salido del cine con esperanza después de haber visto *Fahrenheit 9/11* (2004). Mi voto ese año no fue por los demócratas ni por John Kerry, sino contra el vicepresidente Dick Cheney y el secretario de Defensa Donald Rumsfeld. Estaba con mi amigo Hansel. No pudo votar por su estatus migratorio. Ambos coincidimos en que era una lástima porque cada voto era cuestión de vida o muerte. Al mirar atrás ahora, no sé qué diferencia habría supuesto si el senador John Kerry hubiera sido presidente de Estados Unidos. Pero éramos niños en aquel entonces que creíamos en la democracia. Baldwin dice que es sólo cuestión de tiempo antes de que uno se vea obligado a <<reconocer que el mayor esfuerzo de nuestro país hasta hoy no es cambiar una situación, sino parecer que lo hemos hecho>>.

~

En su libro *Behold a Pale Horse*, Milton William <<Bill>> Cooper afirma: <<Durante muchos años, el Gobierno Secreto ha estado importando drogas y vendiéndolas a la gente, principalmente a los pobres y a las minorías. Se pusieron en

marcha programas de bienestar social para crear un elemento dependiente y no trabajador en nuestra sociedad. Luego, el gobierno comenzó a eliminar los programas para obligar a la gente a ingresar en una clase criminal que no existía en los años 50 y 60>>.

Mientras fumaba marihuana con un amigo en Amelia Gorman Park, también conocido como el parque de los adictos al crac, compartí este pasaje. Mi amigo no reaccionó como pensé que lo haría. Me preguntó si iba a votar por Trump. Le dije: <<De ninguna manera. Ni siquiera sé si voy a votar>>. Mi amigo habló en cómo estaba en juego la democracia, y usó la frase <<el fin de los tiempos>>. nunca había expresado una visión política del mundo, pero sonaba como todos en los medios de comunicación y las redes sociales. Él llamó malvado a Trump. Dijo que muchos morirán si es elegido. Este amigo mío es un traficante de heroína.

~

James Baldwin se quedó en blanco en el funeral de su padre. <<Mi mente se llenó de una oleada de impresiones desconectadas>>. Tenia diecinueve años. Mientras observaba a los niños presentes, pensaba en "fragmentos de canciones populares, chistes indecentes, fragmentos de libros que había leído, secuencias de películas, rostros, voces, cuestiones políticas." Dice: <<Pensé que me estaba volviendo loco...>>

En ese momento, en el funeral de su padre, Baldwin había perdido el hilo de su propia narrativa. La parte del cerebro que da comienzo y final a la vida. Esa cosa entre las orejas que te ayuda a determinar el final. Esto es lo que me pasa cuando intento meditar o cuando intento dormir.

~

En *The White Album*, Joan Didion escribe sobre el momento en que <<comencé a dudar de las premisas de todas las historias que me había contado a mí misma, una condición común pero que me resultaba preocupante>>. Comparte un informe psiquiátrico, los resultados de la prueba de Apercepción Temática. Donde se describe la <<visión fundamentalmente pesimista, fatalista y depresiva>> que tenía del mundo que la rodeaba>>. La primera vez que leí este ensayo, estaba en la universidad. La profesora Yood, de Lehman College, me dio su copia usada. Entonces, me sorprendió lo peculiar que sonaba su voz. Al leerlo ahora, a dos meses de cumplir cuarenta, el colapso mental de Didion parece universal.

A esta edad, leo *The White Album* y *Notes of a Native Son* como dos personas que navegan por la salud mental durante los últimos tiempos. Didion escribe: <<Vivimos enteramente, especialmente si somos escritores, por la imposición de una

línea narrativa sobre imágenes dispersas, por las <<ideas>> con las que hemos aprendido a congelar la fantasmagoría cambiante que es nuestra experiencia actual>>.

Esto me hace desear una historia que explique cómo el mundo llegó a ser como es ahora. ¿Cómo se produjo el incendio esta vez, en este momento presente? ¿Por qúe sufrimos tantos? ¿Cómo podemos ser testigos de un genocidio sin perder el sueño? Cuando intento averiguar cómo logro dormir después de rostros palestinos muertos, me duermo. Sin embargo, no son los rostros de los bebés palestinos muertos los que me atormentan, sino mi incapacidad de seguir lunchando después de casi un año de rostros muertos.

~

De *Behold a Pale Horse*: <<El SIDA se introdujo en la población estadounidense en 1978, cuando el Centro para el Control de Enfermedades realizó ensayos de la vacuna contra la hepatitis B en New York, San Francisco y otras cuatro ciudades estadounidenses... Como se pretendía diezmar a grandes poblaciones, la élite gobernante decidió apuntar a los elementos <indeseables> de la sociedad. Los objetivos específicos fueron las poblaciones afroamericana, hispana y homosexual>>.

En muchas noches, esto parece plausible, incluso después de leer sobre el escritor Milton William Cooper. Él era un

antisemita que afirmaba que el presidente John F. Kennedy fue asesinado porque iba a exponer que los extraterrestres estaban tomando el control del planeta Tierra.

Agentes del condado Apache intentaron arrestar a Cooper en su casa de Eagar, Arizona, el 5 de noviembre de 2001, por agresión y poner en peligro a otros. Se produjo un tiroteo, y Cooper fue asesinado después de dispararle a un agente en la cabeza.

Behold a Pale Horse es el libro ideal para todo aquel que ve el final en todas partes y el significado en ninguna.

Me parece que los Cuatro Jinetes han estado galopando desde el comienzo de este país. La visión de uno no es como un telón que se levanta en un escenario. La visión de uno no tiene nada que ver con los ojos, sino con llegar a una edad. En algún momento, los varios sustos repentinos que creías que eran únicos se convierten en coincidencias. Hasta que un día, esas coincidencias se convierten en un patrón. Las ves en todas partes en el mapa de tu vida. Los Cuatro Jinetes siempre han estado ahí, toda tu vida ha sido un final prolongado, solo que sabes que tienes la lente del tiempo a través de la cual ver. No es una aparición, sino notar lo mundano.

Y entonces, un día, mi hija de diez años me pregunta: << ¿Por qué pasó esto?>> Bebés muertos desenterrados de entre los escombros. No sé qué decirle a mi hija ni por dónde empezar. Pero sé que empezó mucho antes del 7 de octubre de 2023.

~

En *Down at the Cross: Letter from a Region in My Mind*, Baldwin escribe que, a los catorce años, para él, <<la escuela empezó a revelarse... como un juego de niños que uno no podía ganar... ya no me hacía ilusiones sobre lo que una educación podía hacer por mí; ya había conocido a demasiado personal de mantenimiento graduados de la universidad...>>

Estos jóvenes saben que un diploma de secundaria no significa nada. Si eres rico y abandonas la escuela, no importa. Si eres pobre y te gradúas, no importa.

Les digo que al menos terminen la secundaria. Cuando muestran alguna curiosidad por una educación superior, se la vendo. Les digo que es un mundo diferente, un mundo más seguro. Les enfatizo que nunca, nunca, nunca, nunca, nunca deben pedir préstamos.

Así es como logré salir adelante, a través de un nivel de educación más alto. Así que, me proyecto. ¿Salí de qué, exactamente? De mi cuadra. Me fui del apartamento de mi bisabuela. Ahora es el apartamento de mi abuela. En realidad, no me fui como tal; más bien solo me mudé. Me mudé de St. Nicholas Avenue con vistas al letrero de *Neon Riverside Drive Taxi Base*. Me mudé al oeste, cruzando Broadway hasta Haven Avenue por Fort J Hood Park, frente a una escuela primaria. No podía permitirme la paz y la tranquilidad del otro lado de

Broadway, así que me mudé de nuevo. Incluso con toda mi educación superior, no podía permitirme vivir al oeste de Broadway Washington Heights.

Me fui del apartamento de mi bisabuela, pero la infancia que vivida sigue entre esas paredes. Les digo a los estudiantes que pedí préstamos. Les digo que se saquen el diploma de la escuela secundaria. No sé qué más decir.

¿Cuánto tiempo llevo engañando a los adolescentes? En mi tercer año de docencia en una escuela secundaria en Washington Heights, me concedieron el premio de Líder Educativo del Año. La verdad es que recibí el premio por mi trabajo con otros adultos, no por mi trabajo con los estudiantes. Muchos de estos chicos eran inmigrantes que vivían o viajaban a Washington Heights y pasaban la mayor parte de su tiempo allí. El barrio es un portal. Seis puentes. La I95 lo atraviesa. Las drogas entran allí, se venden allí, se consumen allí. Y, sin embargo, no hay ninguna conversación con estos estudiantes sobre las drogas, más allá de <<no las consumas>>. No hay ninguna conversación sobre la posibilidad de que alguien en el salón de clases pudiera consumir drogas y/o venderlas. La única instrucción y expectativa para esos adolescentes era: <<Simplemente di que no>>.

No hay ninguna conversación sobre la posibilidad de que alguien en el salón de clases pudiera consumir drogas y/o venderlas. La única instrucción y expectativa para esos adolescentes era: <<Simplemente di que no>>.

~

<<Se dice que el padre biológico de James Baldwin era drogadicto; su madre tuvo que irse mientras Jimmy todavía estaba en el útero>> escribe Harmony Holiday.

También leí esta afirmación en varias páginas web sin ninguna cita. Esta creencia me hace sentir menos solo. Leer sobre la epidemia de opioides en los Estados Unidos me recuerda que no estoy solo en la muerte. Este conocimiento no hace nada para aliviar mi vergüenza. Beth Macy inicia *Raising Lazarus: Hope, Justice, And the Future of America's Overdose Crisis* con la etimología de estigma. <<En la antigua Roma, cuando los torturadores marcaban a una persona esclavizada con un hierro candente, la cicatriz que dejaba se llamaba estigma>> En la Edad Media, significaba las heridas que el gobierno dejó en el cuerpo de Jesús. En el siglo XVII, vergüenza y estigma se usaban indistintamente.

Macy escribe: <<Resulta evidente, entonces, que a las personas estigmatizadas se las etiqueta y juzga como irredimibles, como arruinadas. Los drogadictos suelen reaccionar al estigma excluyéndose a sí mismos de la vida

pública. Lo hacen, en parte, porque las drogas les hacen sentir bien cuando el mundo real no. Las drogas los ayudan a olvidar, dejar de lado y adormecer sus sentimientos de vergüenza en un efecto de bucle que exacerba los mismos comportamientos que la sociedad inicialmente les reprochó. De esta manera, la muerte social puede convertirse en muerte literal>>.

Durante mucho tiempo, me avergoncé de mi madre. Me avergoncé de mi padrastro. Esta vergüenza no tiene nada que ver con ninguno de ellos. Tiene que ver conmigo, con cómo me percibes. Puedes ser un extraño que consume drogas o un amigo de la infancia cuyo hermano y primo sufrieron una sobredosis. No importa quién seas.

Mi padrastro me envió un mensaje de texto diciendo que era una emergencia. La emergencia era dinero. Por teléfono, me dijo que acababa de salir de rehabilitación y necesitaba dinero para volver a casa. Me preguntó si podía enviarle dinero a su cuenta de *Chime* porque no tenía *CashApp* ni *Zelle*. Descargué la aplicación de *Chime* y creé una cuenta, pero no pude enviarle el dinero. Hablamos por teléfono tratando de encontrar una manera. Me comuniqué con mi hermana menor, y le pregunté si tenía una cuenta de *Chime*. Ella dijo que él solo usaría el dinero para comprar drogas. Le dije que ya lo sabía.

Mi padrastro dijo que necesitaba el dinero para llegar a la casa de su madre en Jersey City. Así que le dije que podía pedirle un *Lyft* a la dirección de su madre. Me comuniqué con

mi hermana para asegurarme de que la dirección que mi padrastro me dio era la de su madre. Lo comprobé, la dirección que me dio mi padrastro era de hecho la de su madre. Cuando les cuento esta historia a amigos de la infancia, sobrevivientes del negocio de las drogas, me aseguro de no sonar demasiado serio, para que suene como un chiste y no como un final. Estos amigos son hijos e hijas de traficantes y consumidores de drogas, algunos de los cuales han sufrido una sobredosis. Han sufrido lo suficiente como para encontrar humor en el abuso de sustancias. La aplicación *Lyft* muestra un pequeño automóvil que sigue una línea violeta que termina en la casa de la madre de mi padrastro. Y luego algo le sucede a la línea violeta. Esta se mueve y termina en un lugar diferente. El pequeño automóvil gira a la derecha. El destino final ya no es la casa de la madre de mi padrastro.

En esta parte de la historia, suelo decir: <<Cuando vi que la dirección había cambiado de la casa de su madre a una calle Martin Luther King, sabía que estaba en problemas>>.

Siempre acierta — esa parte siempre provoca risas.

Después de esto, aprendo a hablar sobre el abuso de sustancias de mi padrastro con amigos de la infancia que conocen los detalles. Nunca hablamos de ello abiertamente. Nos reímos. Hago reír a mi hermana, Mati. Hago reír a Alexo. Casi hago reír a Abe. Solo Abe duda antes de sonreír.

Cuando el conductor de *Lyft* llega para recoger a mi padrastro, le escribo: <<Está frente al *Dunkin*. Avísame cuando llegues a casa>>.

Él responde:<<Estoy en el taxi>>.

Le respondí: <<Hablemos este fin de semana ███████.
Esto me está desconcertando>>.

Él: <<No te preocupes, gracias por el aventón>>.

Yo: <<Te quiero ████████. Sé amable con tu mamá>>.

Él: <<Nah, a la mierda con eso. Siempre intento estar ahí para todos, pero cuando pido algo, todos buscan razones para no ayudarme».

Yo:<< Habla menos ████████ >>.

~

Tal vez mi obsesión por lograr que los adolescentes reflexionaran sobre sí mismos era la proyección de mis propias necesidades reprimidas. Tal vez mi cautela con ese terapeuta era una manera de proteger a mi niño interior. Si me dejaban libre, ¿quién sería yo? Excepto un hombre de cuarenta años responsable de sí mismo y de su hija.

Estoy muy apegado al alumno de quinto grado que escribió la historia de un niño cuyos padres guardaban un secreto: eran vampiros. Mi caligrafía siempre ha sido una mierda. En la escuela primaria, la caligrafía (prolijidad y pocas marcas de borrador) garantizaba que tu trabajo tuviera un lugar en el tablón de anuncios. A los diez años, comprendí que todos los profesores valoraban la presentación y la forma

de la botella por encima del líquido que contenía. Pero algo cambió en octubre de 1994.

Ese otoño, la Sra. Arroyo, mi maestra de quinto grado, me pidió que revisara mi cuento corto de Halloween. Su única edición fue el final. El original terminaba con un giro a lo M. Night Shyamalan donde los padres no eran vampiros en realidad, sino que solo le estaban gastando una broma al narrador. La Sra. Arroyo me pidió que lo reescribiera. Ella enfatizó la palabra "ordenado" en su pedido. Lo reescribí y ella me pidió que lo reescribiera nuevamente. Lo reescribí una segunda vez, y ella revisó la historia escrita a mano nuevamente. Sé que quería que lo reescribiera, pero aceptó la historia esa tercera vez. En el tablón de anuncios, mi historia se destacaba a primera vista debido a la caligrafía. Las líneas inestables que formaban las letras revelaban mi incertidumbre. Sospecha ante mi misma certeza de pensamiento. Desde quinto grado, he estado convencido de que soy un escritor.

No fue hasta 2020, el año en que la mayor parte del mundo se paralizó debido a la pandemia, que me di cuenta de que la mayoría de las personas leen para encontrar respuestas que ya residen en su interior. Ese mismo año dejé el Departamento de Educación. Ese año, publiqué *On the Tip of Your Mother's Tongue*. Siempre he sido lector, pero daba por sentado que otros lectores no buscan preguntas en sus lecturas, sino respuestas. Me viene a la mente Chéjov.

Las personas que leen *On the Tip of My Mother's Tongue*

quieren respuestas sobre mi madre. Sus preguntas tienen tanto que ver con su curiosidad como con su propia relación con sus madres. En mis respuestas, omito mi experiencia y mi relación con mi madre. Mi escritura no me ayudó mucho a entender eso. En *The White Album*, Didion admite: <<escribir todavía no me ha ayudado a ver lo que significa>>.

~

Estaba trabajando como especialista en ingreso de datos para una organización sin fines de lucro en Queens cuando me enteré de que mi bisabuela había muerto. Días antes, en la República Dominicana, ella me había dicho, en su lecho de muerte, <<cuida esa loca>>. Cuando recibí la noticia de la muerte de mi bisabuela, salí temprano del trabajo y caminé desde Queens hasta Manhattan, parando solo en una librería de libros usados donde compré uno de los volúmenes del diario de George Orwell.

Llamé a mi madre, que trabajaba como cuidadora domiciliaria. Me gritó, enojada porque la había llamado mientras estaba en medio del trabajo. Me colgó. En algún momento durante mi caminata desde Queens a Manhattan, mi tío llamó. Estaba enojado conmigo porque no le había dicho de la muerte de mi bisabuela. Ella había muerto en medio de la noche, horas antes de su vuelo a la República Dominicana.

Días después, mi madre me pidió que le contara a mi hermana pequeña, Melo, sobre la muerte de nuestra bisabuela. Estábamos en el apartamento de mi madre en *University Avenue* en el Bronx. Me senté al lado de Melo. Mi madre estaba allí. Mati, mi otra hermana, estaba allí. Mi padrastro estaba allí. Y tal vez mi tío. No recuerdo exactamente. Todos me vieron decirle a mi hermana menor que su bisabuela había fallecido. Ella comenzó a llorar. Yo la abracé.

Cuatro años después, fue Mati quien me contó sobre la muerte de mi madre. Ocho años después, Mati me contó sobre la muerte de mi padrastro, su padre. Fui yo quien le contó a mi abuela sobre la muerte de mi padrastro. Cuando murió mi padrastro, yo había experimentado tantas muertes que no tenía dudas de que la noticia era cierta. Estaba seguro de que él se había ido.

~

Leer en 2024 sobre los Estados Unidos en los años 1950 y 1960 me recuerda que el *Book of Revelations* no es un acto final, sino el presente perpetuo. <<Dios le dio a Noé la señal del arco iris, no más agua, ¡la próxima vez habrá fuego!>> El arco iris, la inundación y el fuego están sucediendo ahora mientras transcribo en una computadora portátil, descifrando mi caligrafía en mi libreta de notas.

Leo en las palabras <<la próxima vez habrá fuego,>> la promesa de que siempre puede empeorar. Algunas noches, encuentro que esto es reconfortante.

~

En su discurso <<La lucha del Artista por la Integridad>> (<<*The Artist's Struggle with Integrity*>>), Baldwin dice: <<Y lo que es crucial aquí es que, si te duele, eso no es lo importante. Todo el mundo está herido... Debes entender que tu dolor es trivial, excepto en la medida en que puedas usarlo para conectar con el dolor de otras personas; y en la medida en que puedas hacer eso con tu dolor, podrás liberarte de él, y entonces, con suerte, también funcionará al revés; en la medida en que pueda decirte lo que es sufrir, tal vez pueda ayudarte a sufrir menos.>> Y continúa: <<Uno está intentando salvar a un país entero, y eso significa una civilización entera, y el precio por eso es alto. El precio es entenderse a uno mismo.>> Hay una diferencia entre la autorreflexión y lamerse las heridas de los demás en comunidad.

June Jordan describe: <<Lo que digo es que la máxima conexión no puede ser el enemigo. La máxima conexión debe ser la necesidad que encontramos entre nosotros. No es sólo quién eres, en otras palabras, sino lo que podemos hacer el

uno por el otro lo que determinará la conexión>>. Creo que la máxima conexión son nuestros hijos. Como dijo Baldwin: <<El precio... es reconocer que la mayoría de nosotros, blancos y negros, hemos llegado a un punto en el que no sabemos qué decirles a nuestros hijos. ¿Cómo se habla de las últimas noticias con un niño de diez años? ¿O con uno de setenta y seis? ¿Cómo se puede reflexionar sin dejarse consumir por todo el sufrimiento del mundo?>> Todos ellos son nuestros hijos.

Los años de elecciones presidenciales en Estados Unidos parecen el *Book of Revelations*. La civilización y la democracia están en juego. Kamala Harris, la actual vicepresidenta, ex fiscal, es la candidata demócrata. Donald Trump, el ex-presidente, un insurgente de derecha, es el candidato republicano. La Convención Nacional Demócrata se lleva a cabo en Chicago este año. Me imagino noticias de última hora, locales, nacionales e internacionales; el peor escenario posible: vivir en el fuego la próxima vez que eso suceda. Puedo imaginar a Harris o a Trump como presidente. Imagino a un presidente, un rostro amorfo que cambia constantemente, adaptando su fenotipo e identidad social. No importa el rostro, igual no me siento seguro.

Estoy seguro de que siempre nos encontraremos con rostros de adolescentes dolidos, rostros de jóvenes que, no obstante, sobrevivirán a las noticias de última hora que no dejan de llegar. No sé qué se supone que debemos decirles a nuestros adolescentes. No sé qué se supone que debemos

enseñarles. Sé que tenemos que mantenerlos esperanzados. Sé que necesitan esperanza. Todos necesitamos esperanza. Y no me refiero a la sensación que surge al votar. Me refiero al tipo de esperanza que surge al hablarles a tus hijos como si merecieran saber la verdad. Una vez que les dices la verdad, has hecho tu parte. Hay esperanza en saber que al menos una persona en el mundo no ha intentado engañarnos. Creo en la esperanza merecida.

En el documental *Take This Hammer* (1963), Baldwin habla con residentes y activistas de barrios afroamericanos de San Francisco. Un adolescente le dice que nunca habrá un presidente negro y le explica: <<Si no podemos conseguir trabajo, ¿cómo vamos a ser presidente?>> Baldwin responde: <<En realidad, no es importante si hay o no un presidente negro, me refiero a eso. Lo importante es que te des cuenta de que puedes llegar a ser presidente. No hay nada que nadie pueda hacer que tú no puedas hacer...>>

Nuestros adolescentes en general, y los chicos negros de la ciudad de Nueva York en particular, deberían sentir que pueden serlo. Y que un día, dejarán atrás los mitos y aspirarán a ser algo más que presidentes o traficantes de drogas.

Para crear un mundo en el que la humanidad pueda existir y salir adelante sin importar quién sea elegido presidente, tenemos que hablar y escuchar a nuestros adolescentes como si tuviesen la *World Wide Web* en sus bolsillos. También son testigos que declaran en el estrado. No podemos fingir que no saben lo que está sucediendo en sus

hogares y en el mundo. No podemos silenciarlos por miedo a lo que dirán y cómo lo dirán. No podemos permitir que el miedo a que nos señalen por nuestra complicidad como adultos nos invada. Tenemos que enseñarles a otras maneras de pensar y de ser. A veces eso significa dejarlos ser. Formas de existir en el mundo que creen en lo mejor de la naturaleza humana y aceptan el hecho de que la seguridad no es asegurada. Ningún complejo industrial penitenciario, ninguna presencia policial, ninguna vigilancia y ninguna criminalización del consumo de drogas harán que los adolescentes y los niños estén más seguros.

La verdad es que los adultos no conocen el camino. Por eso, como adultos, todo lo que podemos hacer es hablar del mundo con los adolescentes tal como es, y no como pretendemos que sea. Siempre llega un momento en la vida de los adultos que tienen adolescentes en su vida, en que surge un tema y los adultos tienen que negociar si deben alentar al adolescente a actuar como alguien en el mundo como debería ser o actuar en el mundo como es. ¿Les dice el adulto que pongan la otra mejilla o les revela que a veces todo lo que se necesita es poner la otra mejilla una vez para que el mundo se te caiga del cuello? ¿Le dice el adulto al adolescente <<simplemente di no a las drogas>> sin explicarle qué sucede o qué hacer cuando otros adolescentes a su alrededor consumen drogas? ¿Considera el adulto alguna vez que su propio adolescente podría experimentar con drogas? En ese momento, ¿se da cuenta el padre de que la omisión no

protege, sino que pospone la traición? ¿Cuándo le revela el padre la verdad a su hijo adolescente?

La adolescencia es el *Book of Revelations*. El mundo que creías conocer se va acabando poco a poco con cada cambio en tu cuerpo y cada máscara que se cae de los rostros de los adultos de tu familia. Siempre llega un momento en la vida de un adolescente en el que te das cuenta de que los adultos no saben lo que hacen. Hay un antes y un después en la historia que te cuentas sobre tu madre, tu padre y los demás adultos de tu vida. Esto te hizo enfadar porque, en esencia, te mintieron y omitieron la verdad sobre sí mismos. Y esas verdades sobre ellos les permitieron juzgarte y castigarte como a un dios diva haciendo un berrinche.

¿Cómo hablar con nuestros adolescentes sin una máscara? No podemos ocultarles nuestro rostro para siempre. Tarde o temprano, serán adultos. Tarde o temprano, moriremos y nos quitarán las máscaras. Es desgarrador que la vida de tantas personas famosas se haya reducido a la forma en que murieron. Personas famosas y personas que conocemos. Cuando una autopsia revela que la muerte se debió a una sobredosis, la historia de la vida de la persona se convierte en algo más en la mente de quienes nunca la conocieron. *Autopsy* se deriva del griego autopsia, que significa <<ver con los propios ojos>>.

No hay un momento exacto en el que el mundo real de los adultos es revelado a nuestros adolescentes. Nuestros adolescentes no completarán un proceso de transformación

que los capacite para procesar las verdades de los adultos. Están expuestos a las drogas en la escuela, en sus vecindarios, y en Internet. Prepararlos para un mundo con sustancias que alteran el estado de ánimo, es decir, drogas, diciéndoles que se resistan y se nieguen a consumirlas es prepararlos para el fracaso.

En *The Harm Reduction Gap: Helping Individuals Left Behind by Conventional Drug Prevention and Abstinence-only Addiction Treatment*, Sheila P. Vakharia analiza el fracaso de la campaña de prevención de drogas <<Solo di NO>> y el tratamiento basado únicamente en la abstinencia. En el libro, ella hace referencia a una encuesta de 2021 que mostró que <<el setenta por ciento de la población estadounidense mayor de doce años había consumido alcohol, un producto de tabaco o nicotina, o una droga ilegal en el último año. Y casi el sesenta por ciento de las personas en la nación, más de 100 millones de personas, habían consumido una de estas sustancias en el último mes.>>

Muchas personas están consumiendo drogas por diferentes motivos y, sin embargo, no se lleva a cabo una conversación honesta al respecto. Existen espacios que se centran en el tratamiento formal de las adicciones donde las personas pueden obtener apoyo relacionado con las sustancias, pero estos espacios son para personas con adicciones o trastornos diagnosticables por consumo de sustancias. Algunos son centros de prevención de sobredosis (conocidos como *OPC*, por sus siglas en inglés). Estos centros

brindan un lugar donde las personas pueden consumir de manera segura las drogas obtenidas previamente bajo la supervisión de un personal capacitado. ¿Qué sucede con quienes consumen drogas o alcohol en entornos sociales, los que consumen en exceso de manera esporádica o los que experimentan? Nuestro enfoque se ha centrado en prevenir el consumo de drogas y tratar a los adictos. ¿Qué sucede con todos los demás que consumen drogas?

Según la Dra. Vakharia, <<las personas pueden vivir una vida segura y plena en un mundo con drogas, si cuentan con las herramientas y la educación adecuadas...>>

~

Mati me llamó para decirme sobre la muerte de mi madre. Me llamó para decirme sobre la muerte de mi padrastro. Felicito a mi hermana porque, incluso a pesar de sus adicciones y problemas de salud mental, se mantuvo al lado de ellos y les daba la bienvenida cuando regresaban. Yo me tomé descansos de mi madre y mi padrastro. Para ser franco, hubo muchos, muchos meses, quiza años, en los que no hablé con ellos. Me pregunto si, de estar vivos, hubiesen tenido un Centro de Prevención de Opiáceos en sus vidas. Me pregunto cómo habrían sido los últimos mensajes de texto entre nosotros si no hubiera sentido vergüenza, culpa y rabia. Ahora sé que querían sentirse normales. Drogarse tiene que ver con

no hundirse en el pasado. La ira hacia otra persona que se droga tiene que ver con el control. Estaba enojado por no poder evitar que se drogaran. Estaba enojado por no poder protegerlos de la muerte. Y, sin embargo, eso no significaba que debiera protegerme de ser lastimado, fingiendo que no existían. Antes de que murieran los había borrado de mi vida porque era demasiado difícil enfrentarlos y aceptarlos tal como eran.

Había partes de mí que contenía en lo que escribía. Escribía en segunda persona para separarme de mí mismo y de muchas personas en mi vida. Escribía con tantos silencios porque no quería oírlos. En *The Creative Process*, Baldwin escribe: <<Somos responsables de nuestras acciones, pero rara vez las entendemos... si nos entendiéramos mejor a nosotros mismos, nos haríamos menos daño>>.

~

Mi hija es casi una adolescente. En la última visita al médico de mi hija, apenas hablé. Ella explicó su rutina diaria, su dieta y sus objetivos para el próximo año escolar. Habló claramente sobre su cuerpo y su vida escolar. En un momento dado, el doctor le dijo que, si en algún momento se sentiría más cómoda estando con una doctora, se lo comunicara a su madre o a mí.

En ese momento sentí algo que había sentido antes.

Cuando mi bisabuela en su lecho de muerte me dijo: <<Cuida a esa loca>>. Lo sentí entonces. Cuando mi padrastro me envió un mensaje de texto diciendo que, aunque intenta estar ahí para los demás, siempre encuentran razones para no ayudarlo cuando él pide ayuda. Lo sentí entonces. Mi hija de diez años hablando por sí misma en el consultorio del médico se sintió como el presagio de un final inevitable. Un encuentro inminente con la muerte. No hay duda de que moriré y ella llorará. Pero esa no es la muerte que me preocupa, al menos no ahora. Estoy hablando de que ella se convierta en una adolescente y vea el rostro detrás de mi máscara. Y estará segura de lo que ahora solo sospecha. El padre, como ella me ve, morirá. Mi hija aprenderá que soy el mago de *The Wizard of Oz* (1939). Una película que hemos visto varias veces. La última vez que la vimos, estaba interesada en Dorothy. No Dorothy, sino Judy Garland. Preguntó si Dorothy todavía estaba viva. Sé que, en un futuro cercano, se enterará, ya sea por mí o por el mundo, que la adolescente Garland fue obligada a tomar estimulantes para seguir trabajando por largas horas. En 1968, Garland tomaba Valium, Ritalin y Thorazine. Supuestamente, tomaba hasta cuarenta pastillas de Ritalin todos los días. Ya sea que le revele los hechos sobre la adolescencia de Judy Garland u omita lo que sucedió detrás de escena, mi hija descubrirá la verdad.

Tendré más de cuarenta años, y mi hija será una adolescente. Tendrá muchas preguntas sobre mí, sobre su madre, su abuela y su bisabuela. Le contaré lo que sé. Leeré

Baldwin con ella sin desestimar lo que ella ve entre las palabras. La escucharé como la escuché en el consultorio del médico. Y le prestaré atención. Mi objetivo es darle mi atención; en otras palabras, amor. Veremos juntos películas clasificadas R. Hablaremos sobre la muerte sin divorciarla de la vida.

Seré un padre honesto, y un buen escritor.

Agradecimientos

Se hace un reconocimiento a las siguientes revistas donde han aparecido versiones de estas historias:

The Poetry Project : "Comprando Cocaina"
Post [Blank] Magazine : "Casi Todo Sobre Tu Madre"
Kweli Journal : "Sin un Grande"
Mosaic Literary Magazine : "En Las Pantallas"

Gracias, Josh Dale, por estar siempre dispuesto a probar algo diferente y asumir riesgos para convertir a no-lectores en lectores. Gracias, Anna Suarez, por haber visto mi trabajo hace tanto tiempo. Gracias, Luz Burgos y al equipo de Thirty West.

Gracias a:BMCC, Sayida Self, Maria Kromidas, Jim Tolan, Page Delano, Lehman College: Terrence Cheng, Salita Bryant, Tyler T. Schmidt, The New School, Dale Peck, Robert Antoni, el tHe beRnACulaR kReW, The Brotherhood Sister Sol, Jason Warwin, Cidra Sebastian, Khary Lazzare White, Ummi Modeste, Dominican Writers, Angy Abreu, Mariela Regalado, Kweli Journal y Laura Pegram.

Gracias a mis hermanos. Hombres que siempre están presentes. A Robert Carlos Garcia por "escuchar" On Screens en conversación antes de ayudarme a desarrollar el ensayo. Gracias a Danny Vasquez por sus servicios profesionales de

Free-99, siempre leyendo todo lo que le envío. Gracias, Alexo Batista, por ser el mejor lector y leer por el simple hecho de leer, no porque sea parte de tu "identidad" como muchos de nosotros que leemos. Francis Mateo, su cuidado por mis palabras y su constante puente entre aquí y allá para nosotros, los Dominican Yorks que anhelamos reconectar, es indispensable.

Gracias, Roxana Calderón, por tu generosidad. Llegaste en el último momento y nos ayudaste a crear algo hermoso.

Gracias, Katherine, por verme. Eres la mejor compañera en todos los sentidos de la palabra. Te amo. Gracias, Amelie, por toda tu ayuda y retroalimentación. Tu valentía y ética de trabajo son inspiradoras. Gracias, Mati, por haber cuidado de nuestros padres hasta el final. Tu gracia me ha enseñado mucho.

Sobre el Autor

JP Infante es autor de *En la Punta de la Lengua de tu Madre* y *Aquí y Allá: un retrato de la comunidad Dominicana en Washington Heights*. Es el ganador del Premio de Cuento Robert J. Dau de PEN America y del concurso Wavelengths Chapbook de Thirty West. Sus escritos han aparecido en Kweli, The Poetry Project y otros lugares. Ha recibido becas del NY State Writers Institute, PEN America y The Center for Fiction. Tiene una maestría en Bellas Artes de The New School. Actualmente, es organizador y facilitador del Programa de Liberación en Brotherhood-Sister Sol, una organización sin fines de lucro en Harlem que ha brindado servicios integrales a jóvenes negros y latinos durante casi 30 años.

THIS CONCLUDES THE ENGLISH VERSION OF
ON THE TIP OF YOUR MOTHER'S TONGUE
FLIP THE BOOK OVER FOR THE SPANISH EDITION

AQUÍ CONCLUYE LA VERSIÓN EN ESPAÑOL DE
EN LA PUNTA DE LA LENGUA DE TU MADRE
GIRA EL LIBRO PARA VER LA EDICIÓN EN INGLÉS